# Santa Claus
*Vol. 1*
## COLLECTION

A happy CHRISTMAS

# Santa Claus
## Vol. 1
# COLLECTION

Better Homes and Gardens® Crafts Collection
Des Moines, Iowa

(Previously published as *Santa Claus 1999 Collection*)

Monochromatic Santas, *top*, are pleasant dinner-table company. Placed on low and high ledges, tables, mantels, or staircases, displays in unexpected locations always have an impact.

Size and scale work together, *bottom left*, to create an attractive scene. This tree and Santa are appropriately matched according to their height.

Choose any setting, *bottom right*, any number of pieces, and any combination of old and new to fill your home with holiday joy.

# COLLECTION

EDITOR-IN-CHIEF Beverly Rivers

MANAGING EDITOR Matthew T. Jones     ART DIRECTOR Daniel Masini

EDITOR Ann Blevins

ASSISTANT ART DIRECTOR Carrie Topp

EDITORIAL COORDINATOR Carol Moorlach

ADMINISTRATIVE ASSISTANT Shari Smith

CONTRIBUTING WRITER Judith Stern Friedman

PUBLISHER William R. Reed

MARKETING DIRECTOR Maureen Ruth

MARKETING MANAGER Andre Okolowitz

PROMOTION SUPERVISOR M. Max Wilker

BUSINESS MANAGER Cathy Bellis

PRODUCTION DIRECTOR Douglas M. Johnston

PRODUCTION MANAGER Pam Kvitne

ASSISTANT PREPRESS MANAGER Marjorie J. Schenkelberg

VICE PRESIDENT, PUBLISHING DIRECTOR Jerry Ward

## Meredith
CORPORATION

CHAIRMAN AND CEO William T. Kerr

CHAIRMAN OF THE EXECUTIVE COMMITTEE E.T. Meredith III

MEREDITH PUBLISHING GROUP

PUBLISHING GROUP PRESIDENT Christopher M. Little

*For book editorial questions, write:*
Better Homes and Gardens® Santa Claus Collection
1716 Locust St., Des Moines, IA 50309-3023

HIA Member
HOBBY INDUSTRY
ASSOCIATION

Printing Number and Year: 5 4 3 2   03 02 01 00
ISSN: 1524-9794
ISBN: 0-696-20957-8

## CONTRIBUTING PHOTOGRAPHERS

ERNEST BRAUN: Pages 1, 66-69, and 110-115.

MARK BRYANT: Pages 92-97.

MARCIA CAMERON: Pages 120-121, and 123.

ROSS CHAPPLE: Pages 4, 30-33, 52-59, 156-157, and 160.

SANDY HEDRICH: Pages 78-81.

HOPKINS ASSOCIATES: Pages 60-65, 88-91, 119, and 129-130.

SCOTT LITTLE: Pages 6, 38-45, 72-77, 125-127, 139-140, and 143-145.

MARCO LORENZETTI: Pages 78-81.

ANDY LYONS: Pages 104-109, 146-148, 151 and 152.

BARBARA MARTIN: Pages 46-51 and 82-87.

LYNE NEYMEYER: Pages 22-26.

RICK TAYLOR: Pages 70-71 and 98-103.

PERRY STRUSE: Pages 120-121 and 123.

STEVE STRUSE: Page 86.

## ARCHIVAL PHOTOGRAPHY

THE COCA-COLA COMPANY: Pages 16-21.

HALLMARK CARDS, INC.: Pages 27-29.

WEST VIRGINIA STATE ARCHIVES,
     RUBY SWADLEY COLLECTION: Page 32.

*…But I heard him exclaim, ere he drove out of sight,*

*Merry Christmas to all,*
*and to all a good night.*

# CELEBRATE *Santa*

Uniting people in the spirit of giving, Christmas represents a celebration of life. *Santa Claus Collection* heralds the many wonders of the holiday—the stories of its heroes, the glory of its art—and encourages reflection on your traditions.

Enjoy the stories, relish the pictures, and be inspired by ideas that bring meaning to your holidays. From colorful paper pictures to vintage chocolate molds, glistening ornaments to grand desserts, you'll be delighted by the spectrum of expressions.

Display this beautiful book as a fantasy-filled resource for everyone to share. Whether you read it cover-to-cover or sample a few select pages at a time, you'll appreciate the glow it will shed on your celebrations.

May all of your holidays be warm and wonderful.

Enjoy!

This molded-plaster Santa mask, *opposite*, has obviously seen its share of celebrations, but that doesn't stop it from returning every year to oversee evolving holiday traditions. In the foreground, the Santa with the white dog and sled is referred to as "true," a collector's term meaning that every part is original.

A pensive Santa created by master-crafter Elea Uhl is decked in his holiday best to deliver tidings of joy and hope.

# TABLE OF
# *Contents*

# LASTING LEGENDS

SANTA CLAUS.

PERHAPS NO TWO WORDS

EVOKE SUCH MAGICAL MEMORIES.

EVERYONE LOVES THIS

MERRY OLD MAN.

BUT WHOM DO WE HAVE

TO THANK FOR OUR EVOCATIVE

IMAGE OF SANTA CLAUS?

MEET THE PEOPLE BEHIND

THE LEGEND, AND LEARN ABOUT

ALL THE WAYS WE'VE COME TO

KNOW AND REVERE HIM.

Thomas Nast's vision of St. Nicholas, *right,*
has shaped our image of the jolly elf who fills
children's dreams every Christmas Eve.

# A Visit from St. Nicholas

## Only some will recognize

the name Clement Clarke Moore, but almost everyone knows the poem he penned more than a century ago in 1822. In memorable words that transcend generations, he created the familiar story of the figure we know as Santa.

*by Clement C. Moore, 1822*

'Twas the night before Christmas, when all through the house
Not a creature was stirring, not even a mouse;
The stockings were hung by the chimney with care,
In hopes that St. Nicholas soon would be there;
The children were nestled all snug in their beds,
While visions of sugar-plums danced in their heads;
And Mamma in her 'kerchief, and I in my cap,
Had just settled our brains for a long winter's nap;
When out on the lawn there arose such a clatter,
I sprang from the bed to see what was the matter.
Away to the window I flew like a flash,
Tore open the shutters and threw up the sash.
The moon, on the breast of the new-fallen snow,
Gave the lustre of mid-day to objects below,
When, what to my wondering eyes should appear,
But a miniature sleigh, and eight tiny reindeer,
With a little old driver, so lively and quick,
I knew in a moment it must be St. Nick.
More rapid than eagles his coursers they came,

And he whistled, and shouted, and called them by name;

"Now, *Dasher*! now, *Dancer*! now, *Prancer* and *Vixen*!

On, *Comet*! on, *Cupid*! on, *Donder* and *Blitzen*!

To the top of the porch! to the top of the wall!

Now dash away! dash away! dash away all!"

As dry leaves that before the wild hurricane fly,

When they meet with an obstacle, mount to the sky;

So up to the house-top the coursers they flew,

With the sleigh full of Toys, and St. Nicholas too.

And then, in a twinkling, I heard on the roof,

The prancing and pawing of each little hoof—

As I drew in my head, and was turning around,

Down the chimney St. Nicholas came with a bound.

He was dressed all in fur, from his head to his foot,

And his clothes were all tarnished with ashes and soot;

A bundle of Toys he had flung on his back,

And he look'd like a pedlar just opening his pack.

His eyes—how they twinkled! his dimples, how merry!

His cheeks were like roses, his nose like a cherry!

His droll little mouth was drawn up like a bow,

And the beard of his chin was as white as the snow;

The stump of his pipe he held tight in his teeth,

And the smoke it encircled his head like a wreath;

He had a broad face and a little round belly,

That shook, when he laughed, like a bowl full of jelly.

He was chubby and plump, a right jolly old elf,

And I laughed, when I saw him, in spite of myself;

A wink of his eye and a twist of his head,

Soon gave me to know I had nothing to dread;

He spoke not a word, but went straight to his work,

And fill'd all the stockings; then turned with a jerk,

And laying his finger aside of his nose,

And giving a nod, up the chimney he rose;

He sprang to his sleigh, to his team gave a whistle,

And away they all flew like the down of a thistle.

But I heard him exclaim, ere he drove out of sight,

"Happy Christmas to all, and to all a good night!"

ONE WOULD BE
HARD-PRESSED TO IMAGINE
AN AMERICAN CHRISTMAS
WITHOUT SANTA CLAUS.
MEET THOMAS NAST,
THE MAN WHO INVENTED
THE SANTA WE ALL KNOW
AND LOVE.

# THE MAKING OF A *Hero*

Thomas Nast's illustrations portray tradition, customs, and tales, while incorporating many scenes from his own family home.

Thomas Nast (1840-1902) began his career as a newspaper cartoonist just before the Civil War. Although his political cartoons influenced American history, it was his Christmas cartoons that made a lasting impression.

Nast based many of his drawings on the classic poem, "A Visit from St. Nicholas" by Clement C. Moore—which begins "T'was the night before Christmas"—but he went beyond it to create a lasting treasury of Santa lore.

Picture after picture shows Nast's flights of imagination as he established new "facts" about this curious hero: living and making toys at his North Pole workshop (Santa's elves evolved after Nast's time), keeping a list of children who were naughty or nice, and enjoying the cookies the children left for him on Christmas Eve.

## THE YOUNG ARTIST

Nast was born in Landau, Germany, at a time when revolution was brewing. His outspoken musician-father was stationed there with a military band, but his views clashed with the ruling party. So he moved his family to America when Nast was 6 years old. The little boy grew up in New York City to become a passionately loyal American and an outspoken civil-rights advocate.

In school, young Nast's passion for drawing far eclipsed his academic interests. The time was right for a boy who could draw well and who thought in political terms. Illustrated weekly newspapers, filled with pictures of current events, were just becoming popular. They sold especially well because non-English-speakers—and even the illiterate—could at least understand the pictures.

"Merry Old Santa Claus," by Thomas Nast, includes toys popular with the children of the late 19th century.

One can sense Nast's love of children from this illustration featured in
*Harper's Weekly*, January 4, 1879, titled "Merry Christmas."

"The Coming of Santa Claus" illustrates Nast's creative interpretation of a whimsical Santa's arrival.

Nast's early Christmas sketches, beginning with Christmas Eve 1862, offer valuable historical perspective. This 1863 Christmas picture, "Santa in Camp," is one in a series of pro-Union sketches (1863 to 1865) that contained patriotic symbolism and drew national attention to the artist and his work.

At age 15, Nast landed his first newspaper job. He was working for *Harper's Weekly* when the Civil War broke out. About that time, he also began to submit annual Christmas drawings, many including Santa Claus—a tradition he continued until 1886, his last year at the paper.

### THE POEM COMES ALIVE

The influence of Moore's poem can be seen in many of Nast's drawings. In one interpretation, the jolly old fellow sits by the chimney, patiently waiting for the children to fall asleep. In another cartoon, Nast illustrates the poem's concluding line: "Merry Christmas to all, and to all a good night!" As anyone might imagine this parting scene, Nast portrays a fat and fur-clad Santa waving farewell as his team takes to the sky.

The charming youngsters featured in Nast's Christmas drawings usually were modeled after his own children. In some renderings, Santa hugs two children—or even a lapful of them. In one illustration, a sleepy lad waits up into the night, eagerly watching for Santa. In another, a tiny girl grasps a sprig of Christmas greenery at her snowy doorway and lisps, "Come now, Santa, I's ready."

Nast sometimes charged his drawings with humor. For example, he shows Santa sitting at a piano playing and singing music bearing these words: "Christmas comes but once a year, therefore let's be merry." In a companion drawing, a weeping boy reads the same words in a shop window. Nast entitled it, "The Dear Little Boy That Thought Christmas Came Oftener." Another sketch shows Santa visiting Bo Peep to give her a bag of sheep's tails, glue, and tacks!

Whether serious or comic, Nast's compositions weave a story of one of our most familiar and endearing figures. His visions of St Nicholas have shaped our image of the jolly one who fills children's dreams every Christmas Eve. ❧

Santa rarely charmed his audience alone. Sundblom would often depict a cast of helpers from Santa's workshop—perhaps a flying reindeer, or as seen *left*, toys that children would hope to receive on Christmas morning.

# Today's Santa Claus
## An Inspiration from Coca-Cola

"Thanks for *the pause that refreshes*"

Sundblom sold the image of Santa and Coca-Cola with help from recognizable characters such as workshop elves, reindeer, and a wishful little girl. Two of Sundblom's young neighbors—Lani and Stacy Nason—often posed as models.

For nearly three-quarters of a century, artist Haddon Sundblom and Coca-Cola have furthered the reputation of Santa Claus as a warm and loving ambassador of goodwill.

Travel refreshed

According to legend, Coca-Cola was invented on May 8, 1886, when Dr. John S. Pemberton, an Atlanta pharmacist, brewed a kettle of the soft drink in his backyard. After friends sampled the drink—and gave it rave reviews—he placed the beverage on sale for 5 cents a glass as a soda-fountain drink at Jacobs' Pharmacy.

As the popularity of the beverage grew, the company expanded its marketing efforts. It distributed thousands of free-drink coupons, souvenir fans, clocks, calendars, and novelties, all illustrating the Coca-Cola trademark. Magazine ads depicted people enjoying their favorite fountain drink, with the distinctive red-and-white Coca-Cola sign in the background.

### "Delicious and Refreshing"

As part of its campaign, Coca-Cola introduced its first Santa in a winter, 1930, magazine ad. The following year, Coca-Cola advertising guru Archie Lee envisioned an even more human Santa and commissioned Haddon Sundblom to create a new image. Sundblom's Santa premiered on posters and in magazine ads—and the public took him to heart.

Sundblom portrayed Santa Claus as a real person—not just someone with a duty to perform but someone who truly loved his job. He drew images of Santa refreshing himself in a variety of settings—always within reach of a bottle of Coca-Cola and always in ways that never elicited any complaints that he was "commercializing" Christmas. Far from it—the company received requests for magazine reprints!

Sundblom drew from traditional stories and illustrations to help define Santa's character. Clement Moore's poem, "A Visit From St. Nicholas" influenced his vision:

> *He had a broad face and a little round belly*
> *That shook when he laughed like a bowl full of jelly.*
> *He was chubby and plump, a right jolly old elf,*
> *And I laughed when I saw him in spite of myself.*

Sundblom, commissioned by Coca-Cola, painted the charming holiday advertisement, *above left,* in 1931.

Santa Claus (Lou Prentice) poses, *left,* with artist Sundblom and two of his little elfin friends.

Sundblom painted his last Santa Claus for Coca-Cola in 1966, but the tradition continues with reprints of the classic Sundblom series in today's advertisements.

Sundblom knew how great
Santa's duties were, but he also
believed Santa loved his job.

Sundblom's images of Santa and friends were always endearing and magical, *left*. He often captured Santa during a moment of relaxation—sometimes with his boots kicked off—and always drinking an ice-cold Coca-Cola, *below*.

## A LASTING LEGACY

When Sundblom died in 1976, Coca-Cola never tried to replace him. Instead, the company continued to reprint the classic ads and salute his work with other memorabilia, including Coca-Cola Santa ornaments, animated figures, and collectible gift bags.

Clearly, Sundblom had created a character with whom people could identify. As Coca-Cola advertising continued over the next 35 years, three generations of Americans eagerly awaited the Coca-Cola Santa Claus to see what he would be doing next.

## A RECOGNIZED TALENT

Born in 1899, Sundblom grew up in Chicago, the youngest of nine children of a Swedish-American family. After training at the Art Institute of Chicago and an apprenticeship with the Charles Evereth Johnson Studio, Sundblom opened his own studio in the mid-1920s from which he began producing advertising pieces for The Coca-Cola Company through the D'Arcy Advertising Agency. Working for several other high-profile companies—including Nabisco, Palmolive, and Ralston-Purina—he was an in-demand artist of his time, earning from $700 to $1,000 per painting.

For a decade, Sundblom based his Santa drawings on real-life model and retired salesman Lou Prentice. After Prentice passed away, Sundblom began using his own face as a model. One year, he forgot to reverse his belt buckle's mirror image, and painted Santa's pants in a precarious position. The many ensuing notes to Coca-Cola showed how much the public loved and studied Sundblom's Santas.

Sundblom's work for Coca-Cola paints a portrait of a virtuous and fun-loving America—as true as the works of artist Norman Rockwell. After all these years, people still recognize and appreciate Sundblom's Santas, and they continue to be inspired by the values he represents: kindness, compassion, and timeless wonder. 🌿

# TIMELESS MEMORABILIA

Santa's many endearing qualities
have inspired people to celebrate his
image in all manner of media.
From paper cutouts and greeting cards
to bellowing belsnickles and
salt-glazed sensations, Santa has become
an indispensible decoration.

Paper Santas have appeared as tree ornaments,
gift tags, postcards, and stickers.

# A NEW LIFE FOR
## *Old Santas*

PAPER SANTAS MAKE SOME
OF THE BEST CHRISTMAS MEMORIES.
TODAY INEXPENSIVE REPRODUCTIONS
ABOUND FOR CRAFTING, DECORATING,
GIFT GIVING, OR SENDING AS
GREETINGS—JUST AS OUR 19TH-CENTURY
FOREBEARS DID WITH THE ORIGINALS.

Most of these reproduction Santas are rooted in the Victorian Era and are of German or English ancestry. The sheer variety of images is astounding. Many paper Santas appear with children and are depicted bearing an evergreen or a bountiful bag of toys. Some German figures carry a switch, and many seem solemn if not downright angry. English Santas, on the other hand, are much sunnier. They're typically not as chubby as their American counterparts, but they're just as jolly.

Not all vintage Santas ride around in reindeer-driven sleighs. Some ride donkeys or drive early autos; others fly hot-air balloons or airplanes. Nor do all old-fashioned St. Nicks wear red—green, brown, blue, and white costumes are almost as common.

Paper Santas, *opposite*, serve as tree ornaments, gift tags, postcards, or stickers. As you might expect, many paper Santas are shown alongside children, and most carry toys.

Here's a survey of "new-old" paper Santas that will add traditional touches to any celebration.

## SCRAP-PICTURE SANTAS

Printed in sheets and designed to be cut apart, most of these Victorian scrap pictures were saved in albums. Victorian ladies routinely transformed them into tree ornaments by gluing them to tinsel or spun glass, costuming them in cotton batting, or even pasting them to gingerbread.

Scrap pictures embellished with glitter or diamond dust were popular in Victorian times.

## DIE-CUT SANTAS

Like the scrap pictures, these die-cut prints are silhouettes machine-cut from their backgrounds. Heavier than scrap-picture Santas, they're made of cardboard and often are quite large. Some serve double duty as Advent calendars or under-the-tree decorations. Others are made with an easel back for display on a table or windowsill. Small die-cut Santas also work well as tree ornaments and gift tags.

## STICKER SANTAS

Seals to lick weren't widely available until the 1920s; the self-adhesive kind appeared much later. Available today on rolls and sheets or in books, vintage reproduction stickers are a no-mess way to create festive stationery, place cards, gift tags, and ornaments.

## GREETING-CARD SANTAS

The turn of the century was the golden age of postcards. Christmas greetings usually imitated pull-down and pop-out Victorian valentines. On the most lavish German cards, Santa was draped in beautiful hand-pasted silk suits. "Deluxe" cards were adorned with glitter and gold or tinsel trim. Other variations included changing-picture cards adapted from Victorian children's books, die-cut cards, and cards with movable parts.

## SANTA BOOKS

A century ago, vintage children's books were so valued that they were displayed under the tree on Christmas morning. Today their reproductions are equally appreciated. Perhaps most revered is Clement Moore's classic poem "A Visit from St. Nicholas" ("T'was the night before Christmas..."), which didn't appear in book form until 25 years after the author wrote it for his children in 1823. Since then, publishers—and illustrators—have created their own versions, a sizable number of which have been reproduced. Other classic books such as *Christmas Dreams* by Louisa May Alcott, *All About Santa, Here Comes Santa, Around the World with Santa,* and *Kris Kringle,* teach meaningful holiday lessons.

## NOVELTY SANTAS

Although today's manufacturers impose Santa's image on refrigerator magnets, wearable buttons, and greeting-card and mistletoe holders, yesterday's manufacturers were just as ambitious with their Santa hand fans and candy containers. Cornucopias were favorite candy holders often made at home. Pressed paper or paper pulp from the 1930s has the look and feel of papier-mâché.

As printing and die-cutting techniques evolve, paper Santas will continue their annual "flight" off the shelves. Start your own collection of these vintage images— whether new or authentic, their charm and versatility will spread warmth wherever they land. 🍃

# Glad Tidings

## Innovative Designs

ELEVATED CHRISTMAS CARDS
FROM A SIMPLE CRAFT TO A
FULL-FLEDGED ART FORM IN
19TH-CENTURY AMERICA.

⌒

More than 150 years ago, a London businessman named Henry Cole had a simple wish: to send holiday greetings to friends and associates on preprinted cards. Cole commissioned an artist to design the piece, a triptych that depicted holiday revelers and patrons helping the needy. Below the center image, a printed message read, "A Merry Christmas and a Happy New Year to You."

The 10", die-cut Victorian scrap, *above left*, served as both a card and an ornament. Woolson Spice Company offered the 1880s card, *above right*, with its Lion Coffee. Because color printing was still a novelty, the promise of a "beautiful picture in every package" was an alluring offer.

Cole may not have known it at the time, but his Christmas card was a first. Within a few years, manufacturers adapted his idea of printed greetings, and launched an industry that was ripe with creativity.

Dating from the 1880s, this Louis Prang card *left,* bore two images back-to-back. A master of printing techniques, Prang used up to 20 colors on a single card.

The American Art Gallery exhibited entries from the first competition. A year later, prestigious judges awarded first place to a well-known painter-illustrator. According to The New York Evening Post, "It is easy to see that art is advancing in this country when Elihu Vedder makes our Christmas cards."

## EXPANDING OPTIONS

By the early 1880s, Christmas cards had finally earned respect; manufacturers then sought to perpetuate the public's interest by introducing new materials, shapes, and designs. For a time, many cards incorporated silk fringe borders, adding a lavish Victorian touch to the printed images. Prang employed 100 women, called fringers, to perform the delicate labor. Prices for card sets ranged from 10 cents to $5.00.

When the silk frenzy subsided, printers developed three-dimensional mechanical cards, printed images on satin and velvet, and added crystal glitter (small glasslike particles) and metalline accents (imitation silver and gold).

Also popular were cards embellished with Victorian scraps, which resembled today's stickers. Workers glued scraps to cards by hand, layering numerous images on a single card. Many scraps depicted traditional Christmas symbols, such as European or American versions of Santa, angels, or birds. Others coupled unrelated images like cherubs and mushrooms.

## A MEANINGFUL MESSAGE

By the turn of the century, German manufacturers had captured the market with penny postcards. American publishers such as Prang—who viewed cards as an art

## RISING POPULARITY

Though Christmas cards originated in England, it was an American printer, Louis Prang, who elevated them to an art form. A German immigrant, Prang settled near Boston, where he perfected color-printing techniques. Because of his work and that of other printers, consumers of the late 1800s finally could buy high-quality color images.

Prang printed his first Christmas cards in 1874 and sold them in England, where holiday cards were already common. In fact, the public sent so many cards that postal workers struggled to deliver them all, prompting one journalist to term the cards "a great social evil."

Prang sparked a similar interest in this country when he introduced his first American cards in 1875. Five years later, he was so committed to the art of the Christmas card that he sponsored annual design competitions, inviting the nation's best artists to compete for cash awards of as much as $2,000.

form and were unwilling to compromise their quality. They abandoned the industry they'd helped to build.

American publishers regained prominence when German postcards were banned during World War I. The standards for their work, though, had long been set by the visionary artists of the 1800s.

Today, the simple greeting card is a messenger of greater glory. Themes of peace, goodwill, art, and nature, are among the traditional sentiments that make greeting cards such a meaningful reflection of our world. 🎄

Touches of ground glass, called crystal flitter, add sparkle to the card shown, *top left*. A German postcard, *top center*, from the early 1900s depicts an Americanized Santa. Much more than a greeting card, the booklet *top right,* was a special gift that contained a story.

An intricate 1870s card, *bottom left*, featured a Santa figure glued to a hand-painted rice paper background. An English manufacturer printed the elegant image, *bottom center*, on silk in the late 1800s. Bearing a postmark from 1916, the textured postcard, *bottom right*, shines with gold foil.

# Der *Belsnickles*

**T**HE QUAINT HOLIDAY TRADITION
OF THE BELSNICKLE, WHO DOLED OUT
PUNISHMENTS AS WELL AS TREATS,
WAS BROUGHT TO AMERICA BY EARLY
19TH-CENTURY GERMAN IMMIGRANTS.
IN SOME AREAS OF THE COUNTRY,
HE RESEMBLED A STERN ST. NICHOLAS;
IN OTHERS, HE DRESSED AS A CLOWN.
TODAY COLLECTORS SEEK OUT BELSNICKLE
REPLICAS AND ENJOY THE LORE OF
THIS CURIOUS CHARACTER.

These vintage German belsnickle figures appear in
a traditional *putz,* the forerunner of today's popular
Christmas villages. This large putz, with an elastolin
house and animals and a handmade oxcart, dates
from the early 20th century.

Four young belsnickles from Pendleton County, West Virginia, some time in 1915, munch on fruit given to them by the families they visited. Note their clownlike costumes and the scary masks at their feet.

Children always were impressed by the belsnickle's visit—he knocked on the door sometimes weeks before Christmas but often on Christmas Eve. Family members gathered around to greet the animated figure—a cross between a clown, Santa Claus, and a mischievous hobgoblin— a lively part of German heritage. Although he was not affiliated with a particular religion, his annual arrival was the highlight of many German family celebrations.

The belsnickle—usually a family acquaintance—arrived wearing outlandish clothes and a mask. He carried a bundle of sticks and bore a bag of nuts and candies on his back. Traveling from house to house, he came to warn the children to behave. Woe to the unruly child who failed to listen; he or she risked receiving no presents from the Christ Child on Christmas morning.

## FULL OF MISCHIEF

Some handed-down stories tell of capricious belsnickles who talked in a made-up language or spoke not at all. They tossed nuts, cookies, and candies onto the floor and invited each child to pick up some. The belsnickle rewarded well-behaved children by allowing them to retrieve the treats. Other children met a different fate. Those who whined and avoided their chores were whacked with a stick as they bent over.

Belsnickles often teased older children by requiring them to recite poetry or Bible scriptures, sing songs, or dance before being allowed to enjoy their treats. Families then offered the belsnickle cakes, wine, apples, and other refreshments (perhaps as a bribe!), after which the belsnickle traveled to the next house for a repeat performance.

Sometimes the oldest child deliberately misbehaved as part of the ruse. The belsnickle would pretend to switch the coconspirator as a message to smaller children who might be tempted to disobey their parents.

Newspaper articles in Lancaster County, Pennsylvania, from the late 1800s recount tales of belsnickle bands playing music far into the night. Other stories tell about the mischievous characters brewing trouble in their communities and generally making nuisances of themselves.

## UNCLEAR ORIGINS

Explanations abound for the origin of the German word belsnickle. Some sources say the word *peltz-nickel* translates literally as "*fur-clad Nicholas,*" referring to St. Nicholas in his fur or sheepskins. Others say the word is a corruption of the term belsnickle, referring to the bell that the character often carried.

As with many other forms of folklore, the original meaning of the term has been clouded by time, and only impressions of the character himself have been handed down.

## A GRAND REVIVAL

Papier-mâché, chalkware, and pottery belsnickle images in various sizes were highly popular holiday decorations between 1890 and 1910. Today, the vintage figures are greatly sought-after collectibles and somewhat difficult to find.

A renewed interest in the tradition of the belsnickle has encouraged contemporary doll-makers, potters,

and other artists to create a new generation of belsnickles in a variety of media. These figures retain their old-world charm but are much more affordable—and just as enjoyable.

When this holiday season brings knocks on your door, be wary of a little man carrying sticks, lest you become part of his holiday antics. 🦋

Antique figures of belsnickles come in many different colors, white being the most common, followed by red. Blue, purple, yellow, and gold figures also can be found.

# SALT-GLAZED
## *Santas*

THE RICH COBALT-BLUE DESIGNS
ON SALT-GLAZED POTTERY HAVE DELIGHTED
COLLECTORS FOR HUNDREDS OF YEARS.
MODERN-DAY ARTISTS HAVE ADAPTED
THE TECHNIQUE TO CREATE A WHOLE
NEW CLASS OF COLLECTIBLES—
SALT-GLAZED SANTA FIGURES.

Salt-glazed pottery, often called stoneware because of its hardness, once was used for common household items such as bottles, jugs, crocks, and jars. The technique of firing painted clay at extremely high temperatures produced pieces that were durable yet decorative.

### A TIMELESS TECHNIQUE
Salt-glazing pottery had its roots in Germany during the 15th century, and the basic techniques have changed

The cobalt blue of salt-glazed stoneware *left*, blends easily with other blue china and collectibles.

Salt-glazed stoneware nestles in a Victorian era child's sleigh *above*. Although new, the figures represent various time periods and cultures.

little since then. The term salt-glaze describes the process that gives the pottery its distinctive look. Small silica particles in the clay melt as the piece is fired, leaving a dimpled surface with the texture of orange peel.

When the kiln reaches its peak temperature of about 2300°, salt is thrown into the chamber, where it instantly vaporizes. As the sodium vapor settles on the melting silica in the clay, it creates an exceptionally hard glaze. The pottery also is much stronger than clayware fired at lower temperatures.

Because salt-glazed pieces are handmade, a wide range of glaze variations exists. On some pieces, the finish is smooth; on others, it's dimpled. Still other pieces reveal hatch marks left from the tools that fashioned them.

Although the salt-glazing technique is simple, a number of factors make the process somewhat unpredictable, so no two firings are ever alike. A high percentage of pieces are less than perfect, making salt-glazed pottery very expensive compared to other fired pieces.

## DECORATIVE APPEAL

Why are salt-glazed Santas so appealing? Some collectors value salt-glazed stoneware because of its history and handmade look. Bold cobalt markings and an absence of defects and hairline cracks are signs of quality stoneware. Whether old or new, the piece should produce a ring when tapped on the rim, rather than a dull-sounding thud. (If it thuds, it's cracked.)

Salt-glazed Santas also are unique for their nontraditional cobalt-blue color. They're welcome alternative holiday decorations where traditional reds and greens don't fit the color scheme. The pieces also complement antique furnishings.

## GROWING DEMAND

Although antique salt-glazed containers are widely appreciated today, antique salt-glazed Santas don't really exist. Many contemporary potters form their Santas in old chocolate molds so the figures appear to be antiques; other Santas are original designs. To add to the array, some potters personalize their Santa figures or even create custom designs upon request.

Salt-glazed Santas open up a whole new avenue for collectors and afford retailers and manufacturers new seasonal selling opportunities. Many collectors eagerly anticipate annual releases—and high demand requires that they order early.

Salt-glazed Santas don't yet command the astronomical prices of antique salt-glazed pieces. Still, their value is enhanced by the amount of molded, rather than painted-on, detail they exhibit. For example, a Santa holding a shaped-clay candle is more valuable than one of the same size with only a painted-on candle. Limited editions also make the pieces more desirable.

Only time will tell how salt-glazed Santas will fare in the future. Yet, judging by the popularity of other salt-glazed pieces, it's likely that they'll survive—and continue to spread their special kind of joy. Whether they're perched on a mantel during the holidays or displayed year-round, their shiny finishes reflect a special light that perhaps is a sign that someone's watching. ✺

*Below*, a new category of collectible Santas has emerged, and the traditional colors of Christmas may never be the same.

# DEVOTED COLLECTORS

~

WHEN CHRISTMAS APPROACHES,
WE WANT TO HOLD ONTO IT—AND EVERYTHING
IT EMBODIES: THE INNOCENT DREAMS,
THE MAGICAL MOMENTS, AND THE BLESSINGS
AND WARMTH OF FAMILY AND FRIENDS.
WITH AN ENTHUSIASM THAT GLOWS FAR BEYOND
THE HOLIDAYS, THESE COLLECTORS KEEP
CHRISTMAS CLOSE TO THEIR HEARTS.

Barb Forbes' display of House of Hatten
Santas complements her extensive vintage
Santa collection.

Old treasures mean new business to antiques dealers
Barb and Jim Forbes. But both prize their collection of Santas,
St. Nicks, and Father Christmases—whether old or new.

# *Growing Up* WITH *Santa*

THERE'S NO SUCH THING AS AN OFF-LIMITS SANTA
IN THE MAGICAL IOWA HOME OF BARB AND JIM FORBES.
BARB HOLDS ON TO THE TRADITIONAL VALUES SHE LEARNED
GROWING UP ON A MISSOURI FARM: PUT YOUR FAITH IN GOD,
YOUR HEART INTO FAMILY, AND YOUR BRAIN INTO ENDEAVORS—
AND KEEP THE SPIRIT OF CHRISTMAS ALIVE ALL YEAR LONG.

The hall table, *opposite,* shows some of the finds that Barb brings home from antiques shows and buying trips. She found the Father Christmas with the hand-painted oilcloth face, goat-hair beard, and green robe in Missouri. The roly-polies came from Arkansas. The antique German feather tree displays an assortment of Santa ornaments.

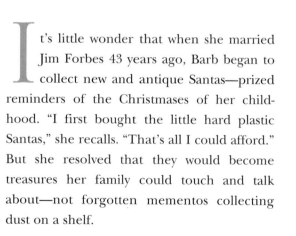

It's little wonder that when she married Jim Forbes 43 years ago, Barb began to collect new and antique Santas—prized reminders of the Christmases of her childhood. "I first bought the little hard plastic Santas," she recalls. "That's all I could afford." But she resolved that they would become treasures her family could touch and talk about—not forgotten mementos collecting dust on a shelf.

Over the years, Barb and Jim have parlayed their appreciation of the past into a successful antiques-show business. Some years they participate in more than a dozen Midwest antiques and collectibles events. Barb searches for Santas at nearly every one. Friends and family know, too, that they can always make Barb smile with the gift of yet another Santa.

Today the couple's figures of Santa, Father Christmas, and St. Nick number more than 100. Other images of the jolly old elf appear on everything from dishware to music boxes to pillows—even on a rock. Barb's criterion for

selecting a Santa is simple: "I just line them all up and look in their eyes," she says. "If there's a special twinkle or glow, that's the one!"

## PLEASE TOUCH

Jim and Barb's children were never cautioned not to touch. "We could always sit and play with them," recalls their daughter, Vicki. "They were never off limits to us."

Indeed, these happy figures have become a springboard for new Forbes family traditions. Every Christmas, Barb fills her antique Santa candy containers with colorful holiday candies. Each of their children—and now their grandchildren—can use their pennies to buy goodies from this enticing "candy store."

Although Barb displays approximately 25 of the Santas year-round, she begins setting out the rest of her collection in early November. "It's my favorite time of year," she says, adding that she spends about two weeks decorating.

descript Santa, add toys and other things, and make it really charming." Barb personalizes many of her Santas with miniature items she calls "littles." She delights in exploring ways to display her collections, filling toy drums, old wool stockings, and baskets with tiny toys, animals, and greenery.

"To me, Christmas and Santa mean love and spending time with family and friends," sums up Barb. "Santas are a bright spot in a sometimes sad world. When kids see Santa, they're happy. And so am I." 🌿

At Christmastime, Barb fills this corner cupboard, *opposite,* with wooden and papier-mâché folk art figures and other renditions of Santa with a rustic or primitive look, such as the hooked rug and pillows. Right after the birth of her grandson Nick, Barb launched this House of Hatten collection, *above,* with the "Nick in a Box" figure.

## ENDLESS JOY

Barb arranges her Santas differently every year—from rustic folk-art figures and playful roly-polies to distinguished Vaillancourt and House of Hatten creations. Garlands of greenery, themed Christmas trees, hundreds of miniature lights, antique toys and ornaments, and lots and lots of Santas fill tabletops, shelves, and cabinets in every room of the house—even the bathroom.

"My mother loves toys and has never really finished growing up," says Vicki, laughing. "Her house is like walking into a fairyland every year. She can take a non-

"TO ME, CHRISTMAS AND SANTA MEAN LOVE AND SPENDING TIME WITH FAMILY AND FRIENDS."

Collector Darlene Lesicko's kitchen dry sink holds a tin St. Nicholas that once shaped and cut 21"-tall cookies.

# An
## *Ornamental*
## Christmas

WHEN DARLENE LESICKO WAS NEWLY MARRIED, HER MOTHER GAVE HER
A BOX OF FAMILY ORNAMENTS. AT THE TIME, SHE DIDN'T KNOW WHAT TO DO WITH THEM.
BUT NOW, SHE CAN'T GET ENOUGH OF HER FEATHER TREES AND ORNAMENTS
OF COTTON, GLASS, AND PAPIER-MÂCHÉ. SHE DISPLAYS THEM IN HER 1860 FARMHOUSE
EAST OF ST. LOUIS, WHERE SHE SHARES THEM WITH HER HUSBAND
STEVE AND DAUGHTER JENNIFER.

Every December, Darlene and Jennifer decorate with their antique ornaments, bringing alive the cherished traditions of Darlene's childhood Christmases. "I come from a large German family," she says, "and Christmas was always big when we were growing up."

## CONTINUING TRADITIONS

Darlene recalls how, as children, in the weeks before Christmas she and her brothers often would hear a mysterious knock at the window. Looking up, they would see her father, disguised in a Santa suit and beard, shaking his sack to remind them to behave—or else there would be no Yuletide surprises.

Now an antiques dealer, Darlene continues to delight in holiday surprises. Once an elderly gentleman from the area arrived on the family's doorstep with a plain wrapped package. To her astonishment, the visitor delivered a white-suited belsnickle, its beard trimmed with rabbit fur. He said he'd heard Darlene was an ardent Christmas collector, and he just wanted her to have it.

## PROUD DISPLAY

Every December, the gentleman returns to see his belsnickle and savor the Lesickos' old-world Christmas. "He wanted to find a good home for his treasure," explains Darlene. That belsnickle joins other papier mâché Santas gathered atop a walnut pie safe. Further down, pewter, redware, and treenware cookie molds spill across the kitchen harvest table.

Darlene and husband Steve built this family-room addition, *opposite,* using salvaged materials from nearby farms. Each Christmas, an 8-foot feather tree dominates the rustic room. The 1890s tree is laden with antique ornaments including, atop the tree, an elaborate, finely printed paper decoration that reads "God is in our home" in German.

In other rooms, more than a dozen cherished feather trees display small baskets, tin cookie molds, and diminutive spun-cotton fruits and vegetables. The trees, with wire branches of dyed goose and chicken feathers, were made between 1890 and 1920 and were favored by German and Swiss immigrants. For each one, Darlene has searched out a revolving musical tree stand that plays an old carol.

One antique feather tree shimmers in the great-room as golden-eyed owls, flying wax angels, and dozens of other hand-blown glass ornaments encircle the delicate foliage. One rare 8-foot tree laden with scrap-paper angels, spun-cotton animals, and glass pickle-shaped ornaments presides over the family room. Traditionally, the lucky German child who found the pickle ornament hidden on the tree would be blessed with a year of good luck.

## SHARING THE RICHES

"We're very fortunate to be living in an area where wonderful old ornaments are still available," Darlene says. "People in this area were very frugal. They saved many things that, over the decades, other more 'modern' families might have thrown away."

With Christmas just weeks away, Darlene and Jennifer begin baking cookies—at least a dozen different German favorites—from anise-flavored springerle and cinnamon stars to lebkuchen and peppery pfeffernuesse. They roll out the dough with well-worn rolling pins and then mold the shapes with a dozen or so rare antique cookie cutters and carved wooden springerle molds.

Like the ornaments, they share the cookies with family and friends. "We enjoy going back to visit with some of the older people whose Christmas things we've bought," says Darlene. "And we always take along a box of our cookies. Some of these people don't get the kind of Christmas they used to." But all those who know the Lesickos get the kind of Christmas every good child deserves. ✺

A walnut cupboard in the living room corrals spun-cotton sheep and goats and a menagerie destined for Noah's Ark. Collectible Santas keep watch over Darlene's flock.

Collector Howard Myers'
life-size companion, *right*,
is so realistic that he has
fingerprints and lines on
the palms of his hands.
Beautifully lithographed
tins, *opposite,* offer a
fascinating view of everyday
life in times past.

# A PASSION FOR
## *Christmas Past*

HOWARD Q. MYERS III IS RENOWNED
FOR HIS OUTSTANDING COLLECTION OF ANTIQUE SANTAS.
HE EARNS HIS LIVING ON HIS FOURTH-GENERATION
SOUTHERN PENNSYLVANIA FAMILY FARM — BUT HIS PASSION
AND AVOCATION IS ADDING TO HIS COLLECTION OF
SANTA MEMORABILIA AND SHARING HIS TREASURES
WITH GOOD FRIENDS.

"A Merry Christmas"

A German tea set made for a child is a dainty reminder of the history of transportation. Santa frolics across each piece in a hot-air balloon, airship, or automobile. Small Santa table favors surround the plates, and even the silver spoons are decorated with favorite Christmas motifs.

To enter his house is to step into a nostalgic Christmas wonderland. Howard admits, "I must have around 10,000 pieces." He displays many of his collectibles year-round, but beginning in October, he turns every room into a Santa showcase. By the height of the holiday season, as many as six different trees decorate his home.

## ALL THROUGH THE HOUSE

Santas are everywhere. Artists' limited-edition Santas, Father Christmases, belsnickles, and very old Santas— made of every imaginable material greet guests at the door, usher them down the hallway, and point the way to yet another joy-filled room. Howard knows exactly where each Santa was purchased and when and where it was made.

It's highly unusual to find an antique plaster Santa head with the original paint. Most antique masks have been retouched to cover chips and cracks. The original example *above,* circa 1910, is even more rare because of the molded wreath that frames Santa's head.

Lithographed children's games are sought after by collectors, especially if the games are in their original boxes. These colorful games, made in the last decade of the 19th century, are surrounded by Santa containers that originally held candy.

Tiny glass ornaments, *right,* miraculously unbroken despite their age and fragility, shine like elegant jewels in their original cardboard storage box. A Santa mask, *opposite,* molded from plaster, gazes benignly over a display of smaller figures on the mantel. The Santa with the sled pulled by a fluffy white dog is referred to as "true", a term used by collectors to mean that every part is the original.

Although he began collecting just over a decade ago, he became increasingly passionate about it as he shared his interest with friends in York. "I won't say it became a contest, but we liked to show off the pieces we found."

The condition of some of the glass, fabric, and paper items is remarkable, considering their ages and fragile natures. Collectors would call it ephemera, paper goods that were never meant to last but somehow have survived to become antiques.

In a corner of the family room stands a 5-foot-tall *putz,* a traditional 1800s German village scene to which families added figures every year. At the end of the holiday season, they would disassemble the putz and carefully wrap and store it until the following year.

## Toys, Tins, and Tea Sets

Howard's Christmas collection also includes more than 50 children's books dating from the late 1800s and early 1900s; others are as recent as his own childhood. In the dining room, two nodding store-display Santas sit in their sleighs pulled by nodding reindeer. These nodders, or clockwork figures, are set in motion by winding a clock key to run for as long as eight hours—which not coincidentally was about how long early department stores were open for business.

In yet another corner, brightly colored lithographed tins fill the dry sink. One of Howard's favorites is a tiny

lard tin that shows Santa and his sleigh being pulled by eight tiny pigs. A rare German tea set reflects 19th-century fascination with transportation: Santa delivers his goodies not by sleigh but by hot-air balloon, airship, and automobile. And a collection of cardboard candy containers are as colorful on the outside as they once were on the inside. From the late 1800s until the 1970s, churches, schools, and banks filled the containers with tiny holiday treats.

## Birds of a Feather

To share the joy of this spectacular Christmas show, Howard invites about 200 friends and family members to his house every year. He uses the occasion to serve a sumptuous buffet of his own smoked hams, roasts, and trimmings typical of a traditional holiday meal.

Howard belongs to a group called Der Belsnickles, including 13 avid Christmas collectors who all live in southern Pennsylvania. Each December, they travel from house to house, enjoying each other's latest finds, sharing refreshments, and delighting in favors—always with a Christmas theme. The group's interaction extends year-round to sales, shows, and friendly gatherings where they revel in their favorite Christmas collectibles.

For Howard, collecting Christmas is a way of life—a way to feed close friendships, celebrate history, and share an appreciation for a treasured heritage. ❧

# MANY HAPPY *Returns*

POLLY MINICK COLLECTS MINIATURE
SANTAS, FEATHER TREES, PEWTER COOKIE MOLDS,
AND OTHER HOLIDAY TREASURES—BUT FOREMOST,
SHE COLLECTS FAMILY CHRISTMAS MEMORIES.
SHE AND HER HUSBAND TOM HAVE LIVED IN THE
SAME ANN ARBOR, MICHIGAN, HOUSE SINCE
THE EARLY 1960S, AND THEY LOOK FORWARD
TO THE ANNUAL RETURN OF THEIR THREE
GROWN SONS AND DAUGHTER-IN-LAW.

～

Polly orchestrates the cheerful holiday mood. Freshly cut pine, inviting baked treats, and a warm display of Christmas decorations are the elements she prepares for her family's enjoyment.

Filled with greenery, Santas, and sleds, this family-room addition, *opposite,* is Minick's holiday gathering place.

As a veteran collector, Polly has become more selective about the items she buys and those she lets pass.

A neighbor introduced Polly to the delights of German Christmas cookies. Since that time, Polly's kitchenware collection has expanded to include vintage Santa and reindeer cutters.

When her sons moved away to college, Polly replaced football posters with quilts and collectibles. She hooked the welcome rug, *above*.

## GROWING PAINS

The family's three-bedroom ranch-style house has changed much over the decades. While the children were living there, the house seemed to shrink a bit with each passing year—even after enlarging the kitchen and dining room and adding a family room.

Then when the boys started to leave home for college, snug crowded rooms became spacious again. "We were getting pretty cramped raising a bunch of athletes," Polly says. "Now the home is just the right size for Tom and me." If the couple feels like getting away, they escape north to their vacation cabin on Lake Huron's Drummond Island, where they retreat with their sons for a few days after Christmas each year.

Both houses are decorated with treasures from Polly's countless forays to swap meets, antiques shops, and garage sales. "I started buying antiques when Tom and I were first married," Polly says. "In those days, antiques were a matter of necessity in order to save money."

## NEW ADVENTURES

Earlier in their lives when Tom was a sheriff's deputy (he's now a corporate vice president), Polly's first major investment was Christmas decorations. "I went to the dime store and loaded up on all blue decorations. They were nothing I would choose today, but they got me thinking in terms of decor and arranging colors."

By the time the boys came along, Polly was collecting painted furniture pieces, kitchenware, and pottery. Though she was the buyer, she always involved the kids in her pursuits. "I'd promise an ice-cream cone to the first one who spotted an antiques store," she says. "I found some great shops that I would have missed."

The Minicks spent their sons' school years right through college on the road as the boys' sports took them all around Michigan; and Polly took advantage of the opportunity to discover new shops. She recalls when son, Jim, helped her spot a pine cupboard on an expedition to a wrestling tournament. "He was about nine then. The whole way home, Jim complained about riding in the car with that cupboard. It was in this house for 15 years, and now it's up at the island."

## FULFILLING A QUEST

As a veteran collector, Polly has become increasingly selective through the years. The fun has been as much in the hunt as in the acquisition. "You're looking for something, though you really don't expect to find it. Then suddenly it's in front of you," says Polly. "The other day I found a miniature blue Noah's ark. I hadn't seen one in a year and a half, and there it was," she says.

With just such antiques, Polly has taken the Minick home from ordinary to extraordinary. "When the family gathers on Christmas to open presents, I want this home to be a special place, and it is," she says. Tom agrees. "Polly's the life of this home," he says. "What she does is always kind of a surprise. Even now, after all these Christmases, she manages to make each holiday a little more memorable than the last." ❧

# THE SWEETEST
# *Santa Treats*

ADRIENNE TROUW HAS A PASSION FOR
ANTIQUE CHOCOLATE MOLDS OF EVERY SHAPE AND SIZE.
WHEN SHE MARRIED AND MOVED TO HOLLAND IN 1964,
SHE FELL IN LOVE WITH THE COUNTRY'S TRADITIONS.
SHE WAS ESPECIALLY CAPTIVATED BY THE OLD,
HAND-CARVED WOODEN COOKIE MOLDS SHE FOUND,
AND SHE BEGAN SELLING THEM IN HER
ROTTERDAM ANTIQUES SHOP.

Adrienne admires a piece of chalkware, *above,* crafted from one of her antique Santa molds.
A small part of her collection is shown in the background. Shown *opposite* are three new molds:
from *left* to *right*, a Victorian Santa, the Dutch Saint Nicholas, and a (Thomas) Nast Santa.

When we think of Santa's usual mode of transport, a reindeer-driven sleigh comes to mind. But in the antique molds *above*, he's pictured riding a motorcycle, a donkey, and even a pig!

When Adirenne Trouw discovered her first metal chocolate mold at a local outdoor market, she immediately began looking for more, charmed by the fairy-tale quality of the figures. She was surprised that her European customers weren't familiar with them until she learned that only professional candymakers used them.

Adrienne's collection realized its biggest gain when husband Bas told her of an old chocolate company that was going out of business. There, with more than 3,000 molds, some still with chocolate in them, she found many to add to her collection. Today her collection numbers about 350. "I like different ones for different reasons," she says, refusing to single out a favorite.

## A FANCY FOR FOLKLORE

Adrienne is fascinated by the legends behind her chocolate molds. "In November," she explains, "Dutch children set out their shoes or slippers filled with carrots and straw for St. Nicks' horse. When St. Nick arrives, his servant, Black Peter, replaces the carrots and straw with a chocolate surprise." Those chocolate surprises were molded in hundreds of shapes and sizes, including animals, clowns, rocking horses, and teddy bears. Fairy-tale figures were popular, too. Characters such as Red Riding Hood, Cinderella, and the Three Little Pigs were immortalized in chocolate molds.

One of Adrienne's most prized and unusual molds, 17 inches tall and 9 inches wide, features St. Nicholas standing beside two children in a tub. In Dutch, the mold was referred to as a *blikvanger* or attention-getter and was used for display in shop windows. Only major candymakers could afford to buy these large molds; small shops would rent them.

## RARE FINDS

The majority of old molds were made between 1890 and 1920, years before plastic molds were introduced. The two- and sometimes four-piece molds were made by pressing metal into steel casts and hammering out engravings by hand. That cast model could be used for years.

Older molds are distinguished by their detailing and weight. A majority of them have a fluted flange or edging that allows for greater contouring and three-dimensional sculpting. Other old molds have flat flanges.

Rings or clips on the molds held the front and back pieces together while the chocolate was setting and were easy to release when the chocolate was firm. To speed production, some candymakers soldered hinges onto the molds so they could open and close the molds easily. Professional—but economical—chocolate makers always made hollow figures by coating open molds with melted chocolate. Some chocolate makers painted their molds with tinted chocolate before coating them with regular chocolate.

Most chocolate molds were made in Holland, Switzerland, France, and England. Some of the finest molds were manufactured in Dresden, Germany, Adrienne says. The mold makers would print a number and their name in a corner of the flange.

## AN AUTHENTIC REVIVAL

"Today the old mold supply has dried up," Adrienne says. "When a cast is lost, it isn't remade because of the prohibitive cost." Now she and her husband import and sell new molds made from antique casts. "They aren't reproductions," she explains. "They're made in the original casts so they're identical to the old molds."

Santa molds come in every shape, size, and situation, *top.* Shown are a Father Christmas, a Santa with reindeer, and a contemporary Santa. Pieces of chalkware, *bottom,* stand among their mold counterparts — a Dutch Saint Nicholas, *left*, German Belsnickel, *center*, and a Victorian Santa, *right*.

Adrienne is proud to have introduced Americans to these new molds. "They bring a lot of the charm of the past to the present and remind us of earlier times," she says. "For some people, chocolate-molding may become the start of a new family tradition." ❧

# MASTER CRAFTERS

CHRISTMAS ROUSES MEMORIES AND EMOTIONS
THAT STIR OUR SPIRITS YEAR AFTER YEAR. FOR SOME, THOSE
SPIRITS COME ALIVE THROUGH REMARKABLY REALISTIC
SANTA IMAGES. WHETHER MOLDING CLAY, WHITTLING WOOD,
OR FASHIONING ELEGANT HOLIDAY ATTIRE, THESE MASTER
CRAFTERS MAKE SANTA TANGIBLE. TOUCH A CURLY BEARD,
SEE THE GLOW OF TWINKLING EYES, AND FEEL
THE JOY OF EACH SPIRITED SANTA.

This North Pole Santa, *opposite,* with his red leather apron,
is a sentimental favorite of the artists, Pat and Glen East.

IN NORTHEAST IOWA'S LITTLE NORWAY,
IN THE BEAUTIFUL TOWN OF DECORAH, IS THE HOME OF ELEA UHL,
WHO EXPRESSES HER LOVE OF VINTAGE CLOTHING THROUGH
THE EXQUISITE SANTAS SHE DESIGNS.

# THE VINTAGE CHARM OF
# *Old World Santas*

Vintage fabrics surround Elea Uhl, *above,* as she creates her elegantly clothed Santas. A lifetime of working with fabrics and color started her hobby-turned-business. The 4-foot-tall Santa, *opposite* has real fur—salvaged from old coats—an antique-coat clasp, and details such as the braiding on the cuffs.

F abrics are stacked on every available surface. Dolls line the walls in every stage of completion—some of bare wood, some with batting-wrapped arms, and some without hair. But the finished Santas are embellished with "old-world" finery, fluffy beards, and lifelike faces.

### EARLY INSPIRATION

Elea developed her passion for dolls growing up on a small farm near Grand Meadow, Minnesota. "We never had much money, but there was always creativity and an attic full of old clothes," she says. There she sewed many of her own clothes and loved making period costumes for local theater productions. Small wonder that when she began making Santas she decided to incorporate vintage fabrics.

For nearly 15 years, Elea made her own Christmas gifts. Several years ago, she was intrigued by a primitive Santa made of wood and came up with her own variation. "I sculpted a face in clay, placed it on my little man, and added some old fabric. He just seemed to come alive!"

That same year, she presented Santas to her family and friends as early Christmas gifts. In just two weeks, she received more than 150 orders for more, and by year-end she'd sold about 400 of the 16-inch dolls. Almost unintentionally, she had started her own business, which she now calls Uhl-Tide Creations.

### OLD-WORLD ELEGANCE

Elea prefers European-looking Santas to the typical red-and-white versions, seeking out vintage fabrics at second-hand stores and garage sales to embellish them. Tapestries from draperies, brocades from outdated upholstery, old dresses, and old fur coats are her precious treasures.

A Victorian Santa, *right,* exquisitely dressed right down to his boots, holds a porcelain doll and sits on an antique cabinet in Elea's living room. Color and texture are two important considerations in choosing fabric for Santa outfits.

All of Elea's Santas tell a story and wear clothing appropriate to their characters. "Some nights I can't even sleep without designing dolls in my head," she admits. A Netherlands Santa and French and Scandinavian Santas are some of her newest projects.

Elea's new occupation quickly filled what little free time she had. As the long-time activities director at Northeast Iowa Community College, she directs the Junior Nordic Dancers (a Scandinavian folk-dance group) and sings in the Decorah Chorale. She also coordinates vintage-clothing fashion shows whenever she can. To spend time with her family, she set up her workstation in the family room, where she can sew while they relax.

## BUILDING CHARACTER

As demand for Elea's Santas increases, her family helps out. Husband Randy sets up Santa displays at shows. An

Homespun stripes clothe the Santa, *right,* while his counterpart, *left,* made from an almost identical pattern, is adorned in sumptuous velvet and gold lamé. Careful attention to eyes, wrinkles, and hair results in faces so expressive they seem lifelike.

accomplished newspaper photographer, he photographs her work to use as references once the Santas are sold. Elea's teenage son Matthew cut boards for bases the first few years, but now her father has taken over that task.

Daughter Megan helps roll clay into balls. Elea says they fit right into her original molds for casting faces on the smaller dolls. (She sculpts the faces individually on one-of-a-kind Santas.) After placing the eyes, adjusting the expression, and brushing on blush or chalk to shade the faces, she bakes the clay.

"I never know what my Santa will be like until I put on his hair and costume," she says with excitement. "When I add the details, each Santa suddenly takes on his very own personality."

My family helps critique the new looks I create. They suggest different colors and clothing, and most of all, they encourage me," she says. Elea thrives on the support. Her passion shows in every Santa she creates as she continues to perfect her art and inspire others to pursue their own. ❧

# *Christmas Visions*

## *from the*

# BLUE RIDGE MOUNTAINS

THE ANTIQUE CHARM OF A VICTORIAN CHRISTMAS IS BORN
ANEW EACH DAY IN CRAFTER NORMA DeCAMP'S MOUNTAIN HIDEAWAY.
HER PENSIVE SANTAS ARE FLUSH WITH DETAIL, RICH WITH
CHARACTER, AND FULL OF CHRISTMAS SPIRIT.

Outside Norma DeCamp's hideaway home, time seems frozen. Her kitchen window frames the 28 peaks of North Carolina's timeless Blue Ridge Mountains, looming from a misty valley. Chickadees, cardinals, titmice, and yellow buntings chirp and flutter among the trees. The intrusive sounds of civilization rarely reach this country cottage, which is accessible only by a steep four-mile-long dirt road. Few people are privy to Norma's precise location or even her phone number, and her mail is delivered to a distant post-office box.

Norma often details her Santas with evocative features that mimic Victorian greeting cards. This Santa shares the spotlight in Norma's studio, *opposite*, with another favorite—a pull-toy Old Lady Who Lived in a Shoe, replete with passengers.

Norma's Santas, reflect the fairy-tale quality of yesteryear.

## INSPIRED BY SOLITUDE

Inside Norma's home, Father Christmases clutch wooden arks, trains, and drums. Some are dressed in brown or red fur sprinkled with snow, and lug freshly packed bags of toys. Other Santas adorn a mantel or shelf, deep in thought or conversation with a child. Each is sparked with the detailed vigor of Victorian design—antique in appearance, but alive in spirit.

Norma, a rising star among America's Santa Claus-makers, treasures the mountain solitude and the company of her craft, although she does love visits from family and friends. A busy work schedule leaves little room for unplanned interruptions. Because her Santas and collector's dolls attract so much attention, she works six days a week, usually 12 to 14 hours a day.

## A DISTINCTIVE LOOK

Norma's art is distinguished by its fairy-tale quality of yesteryear. Whether they're large or small, her Santas aren't the jolly, roly-poly, American dime-store variety that were mass-produced in the 1920s. Rather, they're modeled after the serene, gnomelike European Father Christmases, whose searching eyes express generosity and compassion.

Norma's dolls are no less evocative. Some have stern faces, like "the old woman who lived in a shoe", others glow with cherubic innocence. The Santas are cloaked in splendid attire of worn-velvet pants, rich fur coats, and weathered white beards. Sculpted cheeks and engaging glances make these fellows almost human.

Norma molds their faces from casts of antique dolls. Then she paints the molds (made with her own secret mixture) and dresses the figures in elegant fabrics. As a unique touch, she crafts miniature authentic antique-like toys for her Santas to carry.

Norma's scraps are provided by an informal crew of pickers—friends and business contacts from all over the country who shop for her at auctions. She obtains wood from builders' leftovers, cuts it to size with power tools she keeps in a shed, and then shapes the pieces with hand tools in her studio.

## LIVING A DREAM

Norma's crafting dates back to her childhood in New Hampshire, when she began repairing toys at six years old. She eventually branched into whittling, portrait painting, and constructing tree houses and dollhouses. During her marriage, and for some years after her husband died, she worked as a secretary but still maintained her crafting skills through hobbies. In 1970, she embarked on her doll-making career.

Among the skills she's proudest of is changing the size of face molds and endowing them with expressions. Her greatest pleasure is the final assembly, when the finished work takes shape. "I call myself a toymaker," she says, "but of course they're not toys for children. They're toys for grown-ups—happy toys for dreaming." ✖

Tales of Father Christmas are told through ornate costumes, handfuls of objects, and striking faces, *below.*

Crafting from his home studio, Greg Hausman, *opposite,* creates 20 to 30 Santa figures each day. Some of his Santas, *above,* are cast in vintage chocolate molds and decorated with colorful paints.

# A Gift FROM THE Heart

FAR FROM BIG CITIES, GREG HAUSMAN CRAFTS SANTAS
THAT ARE APPRECIATED ACROSS THE COUNTRY. HIS HAND-PAINTED CHALKWARE
FIGURES CARRY A SIMPLE CHRISTMAS MESSAGE: LOVE OF LIFE AND FAMILY.
NEAR THE SMALL TOWN OF HERMANN, MISSOURI, IN THE EVEN SMALLER TOWN
OF BAY—POPULATION: 35—GREG AND HIS FAMILY ENJOY THE QUIET COUNTRY LIFE
IN AN 1858 BUILDING THAT ONCE HOUSED THE TOWN'S GENERAL STORE.

**G**reg sits on his stool—quiet and focused painting one of the many Santas that are now his livelihood. "Each different design has a star in it somewhere," he notes, "which symbolizes a Christmas hope or wish." The dreamy expression and innocent eyes make each of his 25 designs distinctive.

To help shape each Santa's character, Greg enlists help from one of his sisters to give each one a story. One Santa paints heaven with dazzling stars; another protects a "Beloved Child." Perhaps most endearing is *For the Love of Stephen*, the first Santa in a series Greg created to honor his son, who has cerebral palsy. Proceeds from the sale of this Santa benefit United Cerebral Palsy of Greater St. Louis.

## FAMILY FIRST

Although he's often preoccupied with his craft, family is this gentle man's top priority. Greg and his wife Debbie are raising their three sons close to his parents and two sisters.

Before moving to Bay, Greg worked as a painting contractor. In 1989, the couple had the opportunity to

A mystical Santa, *opposite*, gazes skyward into the star-filled heavens. The almost childlike innocence on his face is characteristic of Greg's work. He keeps only a few of his favorites for his own home, where he tucks them inside antique cabinets and arranges them on the mantel, *above*.

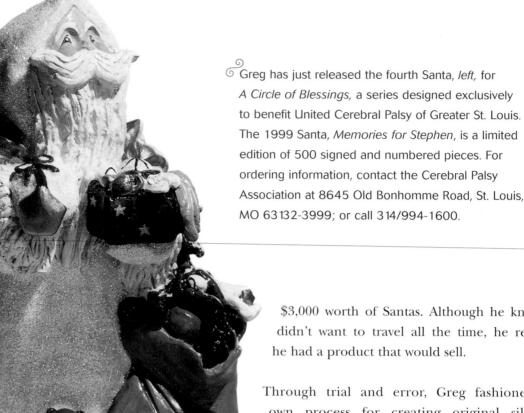

Greg has just released the fourth Santa, *left,* for *A Circle of Blessings,* a series designed exclusively to benefit United Cerebral Palsy of Greater St. Louis. The 1999 Santa, *Memories for Stephen*, is a limited edition of 500 signed and numbered pieces. For ordering information, contact the Cerebral Palsy Association at 8645 Old Bonhomme Road, St. Louis, MO 63132-3999; or call 314/994-1600.

$3,000 worth of Santas. Although he knew he didn't want to travel all the time, he realized he had a product that would sell.

Through trial and error, Greg fashioned his own process for creating original silicone-and-latex molds. Now he can produce Santas more efficiently by casting multiples in chalkware rather than sculpting each figure by hand. After the pieces dry, he hand-paints, varnishes, and antiques them. He also signs and numbers each figure to make them more collectible.

In June 1994, Greg took six of his molded designs to a wholesale gift show at the Kansas City Gift Mart and came home with more than $5,000 in orders. In September of that year, he closed the gift store and began to produce Santas full-time. "I became so busy, I almost hated to hear the phone ring again," he admits. He now has three "Santa's helpers" and sales representatives in 34 states.

Today Greg's expanded line includes traditional Santas cast in antique chocolate molds, as well as his own renditions of angels, snowmen, and other pieces with year-round appeal. The name of his company, Star-Joy, reflects the hope, love, and immense satisfaction he gets from creating enduring works of art. 🍂

renovate the town's general store. They moved in and stocked the shelves with antiques and gifts, hoping to sell enough to make a go of it.

Greg hadn't taken art classes since grade school, but he'd always had a talent for sculpting. So he began to experiment with clay, making one Santa for his mother (who collects them) and another Santa for the store. "That was before I knew how to paint eyes," he recalls. With encouragement from his family and friends, he pursued his craft while continuing to paint part-time and working in the store.

## SANTAS AT LARGE

In 1993, Greg attended his first retail show at a Dallas Junior League Christmas Bazaar and sold a promising

It's no coincidence that this Santa is named for Greg's 6-year-old son, who has cerebral palsy. *For the Love of Stephen* was the first figure Greg designed to help spread awareness of cerebral palsy.

# The *Gift-Giver*

WITH SNIPPETS OF OLD LACE AND SILK TAFFETA—
AND PERHAPS A TOUCH OF ALCHEMY—ROSEMARY VOLPI COAXES
OLD-WORLD MYTHS TO LIFE. WORKING ALONE IN HER QUIET LAKEWOOD,
COLORADO, HOME, ROSEMARY CREATES RICHLY COSTUMED FIGURES
THAT REMIND US OF THE MAGICAL ELEMENTS IN THE WORLD.

Father Christmas appears to have walked out of a medieval legend into the 20th century, *opposite*. His pack-basket of toys, lightly dusted with snow, exhibits Rosemary's attention to detail. Painting a smile on an angel, *above,* Rosemary captures the spirit of mythical characters.

Rosemary began work on her first Father Christmas a little over a decade ago. Mere decoration was not her intent. "I had a feeling that I wanted to put into a physical form and to have in our home," she says. "I wanted to express Father Christmas not as a jolly Santa but as a spirit of benevolence."

Rosemary makes nearly all of her figures' accessories by hand, and each is appropriate to its character. She weaves the baskets for her Father Christmases and manufactures the tiny toys that spill from them; she chips real coal into tiny lumps for her Italian folk character, La Befana, and she layers fragile feathers for the wings of her hovering angels.

## IN SPIRITED COMPANY

Rosemary has been using her imagination ever since she was small. An only child, she enjoyed spending time alone, drawing or making miniature furniture to fill her dollhouse. "I loved to create my own little worlds," she explains. As an adult, while raising her son Joseph, Rosemary made decorative items for the house. When Joseph struck out on his own, Rosemary was moved to brighten her home and the home of others with representations of Father Christmas, La Befana, and angels. You might say she loves them into existence. And if she could possibly breathe life into them too, she would.

Rosemary apologizes for the first Father Christmas she created. The facial expression wasn't quite right, she says, and his garment isn't antique. Nowadays, Rosemary uses no contemporary fabrics in her work. She prowls antiques stores and thrift shops for timeworn materials. Sometimes the mere acquisition of a treasure such as an Indian trade blanket or ornate buckle inspires the creation of an entire figure.

## SHAPING PERSONALITY

No two of Rosemary's figures are exactly alike. She uses rough molds to establish each head's proportions, and then hand-paints detailed facial features with tiny home-crafted instruments. Her other tools include two bandsaws, a scrollsaw, and a drill.

## LOVING THE LEGEND

Rosemary's old-world creations have Italian roots. She grew up with immigrant grandparents, and her husband Gastone is originally from Ceprano, a town in central Italy. His pet name for her is La Befana. Through her family's heritage and by reading, Rosemary learned the legend of La Befana: The magi met an old woman on their way to Bethlehem. They invited her to join them, but La Befana hesitated because she was busy with housework.

When she finally resolved to go, it was too late to join the magi and La Befana lost her way. Now she wanders in search of the Christ Child, giving gifts to good children in the hope that one of them may be Him. Because she stuffs coal into naughty children's stockings, La Befana often is portrayed as stern. But Rosemary likes to think of her as benevolent. Along with a sack of coal, Rosemary's version carries Christmas bread and a basket of apples.

Rosemary envisions continuing the spiritual theme by adding Santa Lucia and St. Francis to her repertoire. "I want to create things that bring people joy and a sense of well-being," she says. "With most of my figures, you have to look for the smile—but I hope people feel it." ❦

La Befana and Father Christmas *below*, are dressed in antique materials and carry handmade toys. The Father Christmas *opposite* sprinkles the night with toys from his lunar perch. The setting was inspired by an old French picture postcard.

# *Sculpting Spirit* INTO *Santa*

JUDITH KLAWITTER'S SPIRITED SANTAS ARE
SPREADING MAGIC AMONG ART LOVERS AROUND THE WORLD.
AT FIRST GLANCE, ONE IS TEMPTED TO CALL THEM DOLLS, BUT AS
JUDITH EXPLAINS, "DOLLS ARE PLAYTHINGS. YOU CERTAINLY
CAN'T PLAY WITH THESE." HER SCULPTED FIGURES HAVE BEEN
FEATURED IN DOZENS OF MAGAZINES AND DISPLAYED IN MUSEUMS,
AND THEY'RE COVETED BY COLLECTORS EVERYWHERE.

This 18th-century British Santa attests to Judith's eye for detail. Holding a sterling-silver wassail bowl, he's decked in a cape trimmed in Russian sable. The goat is porcelain with real goat hide and horns. Judith selects toys to fit Santa's personality. Here she tea-stains a Raggedy Ann doll for her traditional American Santa, *opposite*.

## AN INNOCENT DREAM

**E**ver since Judith was a little girl, she knew she was going to be a famous artist. Growing up near an Indian reservation outside Missoula, Montana, she was influenced by Western heritage and wildlife. She learned to appreciate art both through her mother's oil paintings and by observing the work of their back-door neighbor, Ron Jenkins, a famous Western artist.

In the late 1970s, Judith met and married Paul Klawitter, whose career as a Navy air-traffic controller thrust her into a military lifestyle. She did everything she could to keep herself busy—from burning designs into leather to creating redwood coffee tables and teaching art classes.

In 1989, the family moved to Ocean Springs, Mississippi, an affluent art and beach community. Inspired by Santas she saw there that were made of cornstarch clay, Judith tried to create one of her own. "It was horrid!" she gasps, remembering that first concoction of homemade dough molded around a fishing bobber and a rosebud vase.

## GETTING ON TRACK

Overcoming her resistance, Judith's friends encouraged her to continue. She read books and learned the folklore, and within a few months, she improved the design, modeled after a German belsnickle. Her new and improved Santa had a wire armature, more depth in the face, and a horsehair beard.

This Russian Santa *left*, traditional American Santa *center*, and German belsnickle Santa *right*, represent Judith's early work. The Russian Santa was her first attempt at sculpting with clay (as opposed to dough). The belsnickle Santa wears a kangaroo fur coat.

Every detail of Judith's Santa is meticulously planned. The intricate features of the face alone are objects to be admired.

By December 1989, Judith had completed 11 figures, which she promptly sold at a local library exhibit for $50 to $300 each. After she attended several crafts shows and won a number of competitions, someone eventually suggested that she pursue her work as fine art.

Judith contacted Susie Oroyan, a doll writer from Eugene, Oregon, who invited her to the National Institute of American Dollmakers Association (NIADA) conference. There Judith's Santas were critiqued by superstars of the doll-making business. Judith also got the opportunity to meet Robert McKinley, who would become her friend and mentor.

Today, Judith's sculptures—including custom commission work—sell for as much as $10,000; others cost as little as $35. Judith, once again living in Missoula, Montana, now hopes to expand her line with play and limited-edition dolls.

## FROM THE INSIDE OUT

What is it about Judith's Santas that makes them "come alive"? Judith begins with a reinforced, flexible bead armature, to which she adds layers of foam and batting to shape the chest, tummy, and extremities. Using modeling compound such as Super Sculpey and a set of dental tools, she sculpts the hands, which alone can take up to three days to make.

To create the head, Judith starts with an egg-shaped foil core covered with a layer of clay. For features, she applies additional tubes of clay that fit proportionately to the face.

After connecting the head and body, Judith bakes the figure, sponge-brushes on highlights, and applies the finishing paint and sealer. Eyelashes are applied with tacky glue, as are the hair and beard of Australian lamb's wool. Santa's clothes are "Klawitter originals," designed and stitched by Judith herself from vintage furs and fabrics.

Judith constantly scavenges for toys and other memorabilia. She'll spend hours to find Santa's treasures—sometimes days—sanding, distressing, and staining objects to compliment the old-world personality.

Pounds of clay, yards of fabric, and nearly a month later, Santa comes to life, bringing Christmas spirit right along with him. After eight to 16 hours a day, working over every detail, Judith produces a Santa who bears his special gift of stirring emotion in all who behold him and turning us all into true believers. 🦋

Collecting Santa's treasures is an occupation in itself, *opposite*. Judith scavenges for toys and other memorabilia, constantly adding to her collections of old-world finds.

Pat and Glen, *left,* join a gathering of hale-and-hearty companions on the stairs of their 1906 home. "They're like having other people around," says Pat. "When we sell one that we've had for a while, we miss him."

Expressive faces and lifelike hands make their Santas look like real people, magically frozen in time. With a fur-rowed brow and a pensive smile, the industrious gent, *right,* pours his heart into his work.

# INSPIRED
## *Heirlooms*

To Pat and Glen East, Santa is an abiding spirit. Like figures from Renaissance paintings, their finely crafted Santas glow with gentle eyes, engaging costumes, and outstretched hands. "There's something about them that feels warm and comforting, like you're around friends," says Pat.

Pat plans at least one delightful surprise for each ensemble. Long underwear may peek out from a shirt, or delicate kid-glove boots may warm feet. She sews everything herself, even hand-stitching the furs and leathers that are too tough for a sewing machine.

To Pat and Glen East, Santa is an abiding spirit. Like figures from Renaissance paintings, their finely crafted Santas glow with gentle eyes, engaging costumes, and outstretched hands. "There's something about them that feels warm and comforting, like you're around friends," says Pat.

The Easts bring their remarkably realistic Santas to life in their 1906 Victorian home in Norfolk, Virginia. In the rambling third-floor studio, the Santas recall a range of times and places: North Pole toy-makers; red, white, and blue patriots; rugged mountaineers; and genteel Victorians. "We try to make our Santas look like real human beings rather than caricatures," says Pat. "When I feel an emotional response, I know we've got it right."

## A WHIM TURNS INTO WORK

Pat and Glen became intrigued by Santa-making after Pat read a magazine article about antique German Santas. On a whim, they made one as a gift for a friend. "People just sort of went goofy over it," says Pat. Encouraged, the couple made 18 more Santas and took them to the National Christmas Show in Washington, D.C. They sold every one.

"Even if no one had bought a single thing, the positive reactions I got would have given me enough support to keep making them," recalls Pat. Now the Easts make 20 to 30 of their one-of-a-kind Santa sculptures each year, while Glen still pursues a full-time career.

Previously a nurse, Pat now works full-time on her sculptures. She's the primary artist, creating the basic dolls and costumes. Glen, a physical therapist, sculpts the hands and forearms; he also builds Santa's toys, workbenches, and other accessories.

## CANDID EXPRESSIONS

Pat begins by sculpting a head from polymer clay, using Sculpey, Cernit, or Fimo brands. Sometimes she starts with a specific look in mind; more often, the character emerges as she goes. To capture the innocent expressions, Pat studies pictures of her friends' children. "Sometimes I'll throw away three or four heads before I finally get one that clicks," she says.

After the clay has cured, she applies a variety of paints and cosmetics to perfect the face. Then she adds wool-fleece hair and a beard, which she washes, rinses, and picks apart by hand to preserve its sheen and curls. To create the bodies, Pat places a wire armature in a fiberglass mold she designed. Then she adds expandable polyurethane-foam padding to give each doll its girth and personality.

Part of the dolls' magic flows from their costumes made of worn clothing, recycled furs, and trims of unusual buttons and jewelry. Pat also hoards a cache of old piece goods acquired from a New York collector. Most of the materials date from the Victorian era to the mid-1900s. "Old fabrics have a quality you just can't get in something new," she says.

Pat is inspired by old postcards and drawings; however, every costume is original. Her dolls sometimes don as many as six separate garments. Pat sews everything herself, hand-stitching furs and leathers too tough for a sewing machine or embroidering vintage fabrics to create the perfect piece.

## QUALITY, NOT QUANTITY

Together, Pat and Glen estimate that they spend 40 to 50 hours creating, dressing, and accessorizing each figure. Their attention to detail and quality is reflected in the dolls' prices, which range from $1,400 for an 18-inch figure to almost $5,000 for a set. They sell their Santas primarily at national Christmas shows, but also accept special orders.

Pat hopes the Santas will become family heirlooms for their owners, giving many generations the same pleasure they've given her. "I have such wonderful memories of my own Christmases as a child," she says. "Making these Santas is my way of bringing them back."

Many of the dolls draw from the Victorian tradition of a benevolent Father Christmas, who traveled to the townships with toys for children. The kindly Santa in the *center* stops to tame a snowbird for young friends.

A smartly attired Father Christmas totes a bag of gifts, including an antique German sheep and a bottlebrush tree.

# Jolly Old Men

~

CINDY GRAY'S SANTAS HAVE A SPECIAL AIR ABOUT THEM,
INVARIABLY ELICITING SMILES OF ADMIRATION. THEIR EXPRESSIVE CLAY FACES
AND FUR-CLAD BODIES ARE A FAR CRY FROM THEIR HUMBLE BEGINNINGS
AS LUMPS OF CLAY AND BLOCKS OF WOOD. CINDY PINCHES, WHITTLES,
AND STITCHES HER CREATIONS UNTIL THEY BECOME LIFELIKE JOVIAL FIGURES.

"Making Santas connects me to the past," says Cindy, recalling fond memories of elaborate childhood holidays. Caught up in the Christmas spirit, her older brother once climbed out an upstairs window to give an all-clear signal to the neighbors, who crept into the family's home to leave the children's gifts under the tree. Even now, Cindy says, "I just go crazy at Christmastime."

### TRY, TRY AGAIN

An antiques collector and self-taught folk artist, Cindy first experimented with cloth Santas but felt that they lacked personality. Inspired by ideas in a magazine, she began working with clay.

Her first attempt looked "more like an extraterrestrial than a Santa Claus," she admits. She considered taking art classes to improve her technique, but her friend and fellow folk artist, Nancy Murphy, advised against it. She encouraged Cindy to develop her own style. Now says Cindy's sister, Frances, "people stand in front of the booth and argue about which one is the best."

### ONE-OF-A-KIND KEEPSAKES

Each of Cindy's sculptures is unique. "I don't mass-produce; I don't even like to duplicate," she says. For hours, she scrapes and molds the clay until she's happy with the expression she's created. "I want him to look as though he'll talk back to me," she says.

An old pinstriped quilt back provides a coat for Santa, *opposite*. It's trimmed with cotton batting and shoe buttons. A headpiece of pepper berries and Spanish moss, *above*, sets off the rosy cheeks Cindy Gray paints with her fingertips. Woolen eyebrows, rather than sculpted ones, and hand-mixed skin tones make Cindy's Santa faces special.

After painting the face, Cindy decides what the Santa will wear, selecting old fur, flannel, wool, or quilted pieces from her cache of vintage fabrics. "I haunt antiques shops and flea markets, looking for fabric, buttons, and accessories," she says. As a finishing touch, she whittles the pine boots that anchor the Santas to their wooden stands.

It's not unusual for Cindy to spend up to two weeks designing and making each signed Santa, so she rarely has extras on hand. "As soon as I show them, they're sold," she says. "My folk art is a full-time job, but I love it. I wouldn't have it any other way." 🌿

A German Pelz Nichol grips a woolen sheep and a staff of curly willow in his sculpted hands. Cindy's figures often convey her love of old things *opposite*. Wearing a belt made from a horse bridle, one Santa cradles 48-star flags, and the African-American Santa wears a vintage crazy-quilt coat. The pinecone Santa bends under the weight of the pack on his back.

# Joyous Crafting

In southeastern Idaho, whatever the season, it's always Christmas in the Satter home. Rebecca Satter's curiosity about the past and her creative handwork have combined to produce rare and beautiful belsnickle and Santa figures.

A jolly old Santa in his familiar crimson coat, *above*, is one of Rebecca's most popular figures. This one is called a mantel Santa because it's designed to sit over a crackling fireplace fire. Rebecca paints a face with meticulous attention to detail, *opposite*.

"I've never had any art training," Rebecca says, "but I've always tinkered with crafts. Making things is part of being a mother. Handcrafted Christmases were always a part of our family." A friend of Rebecca's asked if she would make her an old-fashioned Santa, and that was the beginning of a passion for joyful Santa crafting.

## OLD SANTAS, NEW PERSPECTIVE

Although Rebecca had never made a Santa before, she was willing to try. In her magazine research at the library, she was struck by the diversity of old-world and antique Santas. "I always thought the whole world celebrated a short, stocky, jovial guy. But the German belsnickle made me realize that the whole world didn't celebrate Christmas the same way."

Rebecca learned that European versions of Santa Claus weren't as merry as the American interpretation. St. Nicholas, for example, was solemn and stern, a bishop-like, 4th-century figure. Dutch legend also tells of Sinterklaas, who appeared on St. Nicholas Eve to leave sweets in the wooden shoes of good Dutch children. He also was seen as serious and fearsome.

Rebecca became interested not only in European folklore but also in the German culture that was prominent in 19th-century America. Rebecca's favorite character became the fierce German belsnickle, who takes his name from Pelz-Nickolaus, or "St. Nicholas in fur."

According to Rebecca, the belsnickle typically had a big fur coat and carried a black sack. In German communities, a neighborhood farmer would dress up in furs and then rattle chains and throw pebbles on his rounds to local houses. He carried goodies for well-behaved children and used switches to threaten those who were naughty.

Rebecca often draws upon her surroundings for inspiration, crafting belsnickles that are somber yet lovable.

## A BOLD EXPRESSION

Rebecca creates her belsnickle and Santa figures by cutting them from wood with a handsaw. Then she layers the forms with fiberfill to give them a plump, stocky attitude. Rebecca molds commercial sculpting clay because it's stiff and bakes at a high temperature. For the faces, however, she uses cornstarch clay that enables more detailed, expressive features, which she shapes with toothpicks and cotton swabs.

After drying the faces in her oven, Rebecca paints each one with hobby-shop acrylics and then applies several layers of clear, protective resin. She attaches hands, faces, and wooden legs to the body and then row-by-row, she glues on horsehair beards and hair, building in curls using small permanent-rod hair curlers.

Each figure's crowning touch is its detailed clothing and trim, which Rebecca selects to complement her characters. She cuts the fabrics from old clothes and furs that she finds in antiques shops and secondhand stores and then sews them on her old, reliable treadle machine. When she's finished, the figures stand 14 to 22 inches tall.

## ANSWERED PRAYERS

Rebecca's pastime became a full-time business in 1986 when a friend took three Santas and a belsnickle to a Los Angeles gift show—only to return with 120 orders. "I had no idea I'd be able to market these figures from Idaho," she says. "I really didn't think my prayers would be answered, but they have been. You have to look at it as a job, but you can't make it too much business because then you lose the art," she says.

Reflecting on her craft, Rebecca says, "We all have a need to do something creative. That's where joy comes from. If you can look at a funny little face and it brings instant joy and gratification, that's worth more than anything." ❧

Most of Rebecca's belsnickles, *left* and *opposite,* wear fur coats and hats.

# PERSONAL EXPRESSIONS

~

WELCOME THE HOLIDAYS WITH THESE
INSPIRING HOMESPUN SANTA RENDITIONS.
WITH EASY-TO-FIND MATERIALS AND A LITTLE
IMAGINATION, YOU CAN CREATE BEAUTIFUL,
LASTING WORKS OF ART TO GIVE AS GIFTS OR
TREASURE AS FAMILY HEIRLOOMS.

With a commanding presence,
our Stately Old Gent Santa stands
watch over the holiday festivities.
Turn the page for the instructions
and patterns.

# Vintage Victorian

## MATERIALS

- 8"-diameter clear glass plate
- Art print, about 5" tall
- Fine-tip watercolor marking pen in a dark color
- Two 6"-diameter gold paper doilies
- Decoupage finish
- Metallic acrylic paints: gold and white pearl
- Gold liquid glitter
- Clear acrylic matte spray sealer
- Small paper-cutting scissors
- Crafts knife with No. 11 blade; cutting mat
- Brushes: 1" sponge brush; small, soft artist's brush
- Brayer or wallpaper seam roller
- Waxed paper; paper towels; cotton swabs
- Soft cloth; bowl of water

*Designer: Sylvia Montroy*

## INSTRUCTIONS

### Plan the Design

Cut out the art print to fit the center of the plate with scissors or a crafts knife for more intricate areas. Cut around the main motif, removing as much background as you wish. Wash and dry the plate to remove fingerprints.

Study the pattern of the doilies to determine which sections to cut apart to fit the plate border. *Note*: For the plate *opposite*, the centers of the doilies were cut out and set aside. Eleven medallions were needed to complete the border. To fit the contour of the plate, the medallions were cut apart in five pairs plus one single medallion. The tabs were left attached to each side so the medallions would appear connected and to make a continuous border when they were glued.

Move the cutouts around on top of the plate, making adjustments as needed. To lay out the final design, place all cut pieces face-up on a work surface with the main motif in the center. Position the plate (with the top side up) over the layout, adjusting the medallions to fit around the edges. On the top side of the plate, trace around the cutouts with a watercolor marking pen to make guidelines for gluing.

### Decoupage the Plate

Place the art-print cutout faceup on waxed paper, and brush the front surface with the decoupage finish, using the sponge brush. Position the cutout on the back of the plate, using the tracings as guides, so the cutout shows through the plate. Place waxed paper over the glued piece and use a brayer or roller to squeeze out excess glue, starting at the center. From the front, check to see that all areas are glued down. Remove excess glue from the back of the cutout and glass by rubbing gently with a damp cloth.

Glue medallions around the border in the same manner, overlapping tabs when necessary to connect them. If necessary, push medallions down into the contours of the plate by placing a damp soft cloth over the areas to be pressed down, then rubbing your fingers over the area. Remove excess glue. Let dry.

### Finish the Plate

The background of the glass should be crystal clear. If glue remains, clean the specks on the glass with a damp cotton swab. Remove pen marks from the front of the plate.

To prevent paint from flowing between the cutouts and the plate, seal the back and edges of all glued pieces with more decoupage finish, going beyond all edges about ⅛". Let dry.

On back of the plate, brush a light coat of liquid glitter in a swirling pattern around the cutouts. Brush glitter into intricate medallion cuts. Let dry.

Apply two coats of white pearl paint over the glitter with sponge brush, alternating the direction of the strokes between the coats. Elevate the plate so the edges won't stick to the work surface; let dry.

Use gold paint and the beveled end of a sponge brush to add a ¹/₁₆" gold border to the edge of the plate; add more light coats as needed. When the paint is dry, seal the back and edge of the plate with one coat of decoupage finish. Let the finish set for about one week, and then spray the back with acrylic sealer. To avoid damage, don't immerse the plate in water. Clean the surface with a damp cloth.

## MORE IDEAS:

- *Many types of prints work for this project. Try small figures cut from wrapping paper or even motifs from your favorite Christmas cards. Just make sure the design fits in the plate center, leaving room for the edging.*

- *If someone gives you a lovely postcard or greeting card this year, make a plate using a cutout from the card and return it to your friend next year. A gift to treasure, it will forever remind him or her of a special trip or occasion.*

- *Make a plate with a different design each year. Soon you'll have your own (very rare!) series of collector plates.*

The lovely keepsake plate is decoupaged and painted on the underside of the glass. The top surface is undecorated, making the plate easy to clean.

Dressed in fur, this pinecone Santa poses in the guise of a woodsman.

# FOREST LEGEND

## MATERIALS

- ¾×1½×4" pine block for the body
- Drill and ¹⁄₁₆" and ¼" drill bits
- 2" and 8" lengths of ¼" dowel
- Papier-mâché mixture
- 14" length of 16-gauge wire
- Acrylic paints: black, flesh color, mauve, and white
- Small artist's synthetic paintbrush
- Antiquing medium
- 4 Norway spruce pinecones, each about 4" long
- 5-minute epoxy
- Glue gun and hotmelt adhesive
- ¾×4×6" weathered-wood block for the base
- 2—#19×¾" brads
- Brown imitation fur
- Wool doll roving for the beard and hair
- Miniature toys, brass horn, and other accessories

*Designer: J. J. Bray*

## INSTRUCTIONS

Referring to the assembly diagram *opposite,* drill a ¼" hole ½" deep in the top center of the body block and in the base. Using a ¹⁄₁₆" bit, drill four additional holes for the shoulders and the hips. Glue the 2"

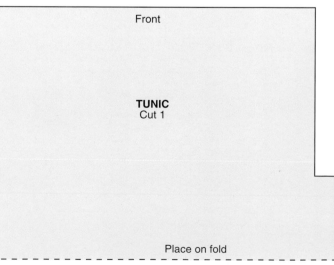

Front

**TUNIC**
Cut 1

Place on fold

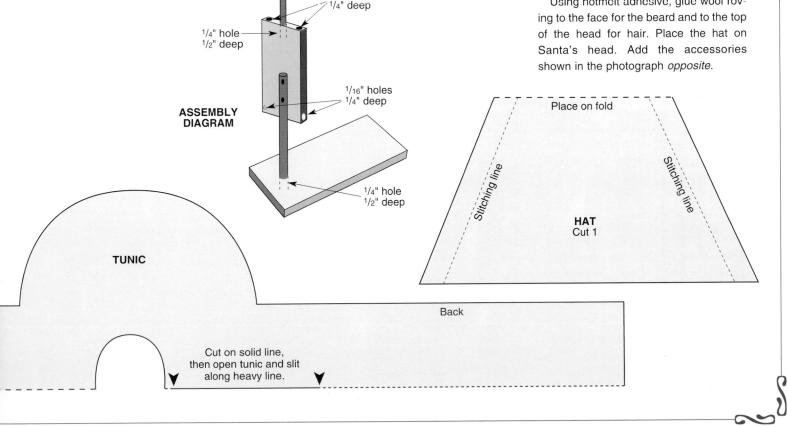

length of dowel in the center hole in the body block for Santa's head.

Mix the papier mâché according to the manufacturer's instructions. Referring to the photograph *at right,* shape Santa's head, and carefully position it on the dowel. Use a piece of wire to make holes for the eyes. Shape Santa's hands and boots from papier mâché. Insert a short length of wire into the top of each hand and boot, allowing about ¾" to protrude. Set aside the head, hands, and boots, and allow them to dry for several days.

After the papier mâché is completely dry, paint the face and hands flesh color. Paint the cheeks pink and the eyebrows white. Paint the boots black. After the paint is dry, dip all pieces in the antiquing medium, and gently wipe off the excess. Allow them to dry.

To assemble the Santa, use a ¹⁄₁₆" bit to drill a hole in both ends of each of the four pinecones. For each arm, attach the hand by coating the wire protruding from the papier-mâché with 5-minute epoxy and inserting it into the small end of a pinecone. Insert a length of wire into the large end of each pinecone, securing it with epoxy and allowing about 1" of wire to protrude. Bend the wire to form the shoulder; coat the end with epoxy, and insert it into the shoulder hole on the body block.

To attach the legs, coat the wire protruding from each papier-mâché boot with epoxy, and insert it into the small end of each of the two remaining pinecones. Insert a length of wire into the large end of each pinecone, securing it with epoxy and allowing about 1" to protrude. Bend the wire slightly; coat the end with epoxy, and insert it into a hip hole on the body block.

To assemble the stand, insert the 8" dowel into the ¼" hole drilled in the base, and epoxy it in place. Position the Santa on the base in front of the dowel so his feet rest on the base. Attach the body block to the dowel stand with epoxy and two small brads. Epoxy the feet to the base.

To make the hat and tunic, transfer the patterns to the imitation fur, and cut them out. With the right sides together, stitch the hat along the seam lines. Then turn the hat right side out. For the tunic, cut out the neck, and clip the opening as indicated on the pattern. Slip the tunic over Santa's head and, using hotmelt adhesive, glue it to the body, overlapping the front extensions and back.

Using hotmelt adhesive, glue wool roving to the face for the beard and to the top of the head for hair. Place the hat on Santa's head. Add the accessories shown in the photograph *opposite.*

**ASSEMBLY DIAGRAM**

¹⁄₁₆" holes ¹⁄₄" deep

¼" hole ¹⁄₂" deep

¹⁄₁₆" holes ¹⁄₄" deep

¼" hole ¹⁄₂" deep

**TUNIC**

Back

Cut on solid line, then open tunic and slit along heavy line.

Place on fold

Stitching line

Stitching line

**HAT**
Cut 1

# FATHER OF THE CHRISTMAS FOREST

## MATERIALS

- 4"-long pencil or dowel
- Thick white crafts glue
- 3½" plastic-foam egg
- 20"-tall plastic-foam cone
- 1 yard of burlap
- Heavy rubber band
- Floral wire
- ¾ yard of 20-ounce bonded polyester fiberfill batting (not stuffing)
- Glue gun and hotmelt adhesive
- Wire coat hanger
- Needle-nose pliers
- Masking tape
- ¾ yard of burgundy velvet
- 1½ yards of gold cording

- Beige peppergrass with leaves
- 2 black beans and 1 red bean
- Rose-color powder blush
- Sphagnum moss
- ½ yard of 1½"-wide lace edging
- ½ yard of ¾"-wide green trim
- ½ yard of 3"-wide crocheted lace
- 6 freeze-dried roses, small ivory and burgundy rosebuds, pepper berries, grapevine tendrils, and broom straws
- Queen Anne's lace
- Pressed maidenhair fern
- ¼ yard of 1½"-wide gold trim
- Sweet Annie
- Foam-core board

*Doll sits about 24" high  •  Designer: Katheryn Tidwell Foutz*

## INSTRUCTIONS

Coat 2" of the 4"-long pencil with thick white crafts glue, and push the pencil into the narrow end of the plastic-foam egg. Coat the remaining 2" with glue, and push it into the top of the plastic-foam cone.

From the burlap, cut a 13"-diameter circle for the head, two 8" squares for the hands, and one 18×27" rectangle for the body. Wrap the circle around the plastic-foam egg, working the folds to the back. Secure the burlap tightly at the neck with a heavy rubber band or floral wire.

From the batting, cut a 19×30" rectangle and two 1×40" strips. Lay the plastic-foam cone along one 19" edge of the rectangle, aligning the bottom of the cone with the edge of the batting. Glue the cone to the edge of the batting with hotmelt adhesive; roll the cone toward the top 30" edge, wrapping it tightly in the batting. Secure the edge of the batting with hotmelt adhesive, and trim the excess batting.

Using needle-nose pliers, untwist the wire below the hook of the coat hanger, and straighten the hanger completely. Fold each end back 2" to form the hands. Center the hanger on the front of the plastic-foam cone 1½" below the head, and wrap the wire ends around the cone. Cross them at the back, and bring them around to the sides. Secure the wire in this position with masking tape, wrapping the tape in a crisscross fashion.

Center the 18×27" burlap rectangle on the front of the cone, with one 27" edge even with the bottom of the cone. Wrap the burlap around the cone, overlapping the edges at the back. Glue the edges together so the burlap forms a tube around the cone. Use floral wire to gather the 27" edge around the top of the cone, and twist the wire tightly to hold the fabric in place.

Glue one end of each 1"-wide strip of batting to the back of the plastic-foam cone over the crossed coat-hanger wires. Wrap

each strip around one of the wires, ending at the hands, and glue the batting to secure it. Center an 8" burlap square over each hand, and secure it with floral wire about 2½" from the ends to form mittens.

Enlarge the pattern on the grid. (To enlarge the pattern, use a ruler and pencil to draw a grid of 1" squares on a sheet of newsprint. Copy the lines in the gridded pattern onto the corresponding squares of your 1" grid.) Transfer the pattern to the velvet, and cut two robe fronts and one robe back.

To assemble the robe, place the fronts and back with the right sides together. Apply a bead of hotmelt adhesive along the seam line of the side seam, underarm seam, and shoulder seam on one side; repeat for the remaining side. For best results, apply the glue in 6"-long beads, and let the glue cool completely before you turn the robe right side out. Turn up the hem ¾", and glue it in place. Put the robe on the figure. Fold the center front robe edges under, and glue them to the burlap, creating an opening that lets the burlap show. Tie gold cording just under the arms to make a belt.

Cut the peppergrass into pieces 1" to 3" long. Glue the 3" pieces to the front of the robe in the beard area, beginning at the bottom of the beard and overlapping the stems as you work toward the face. As you approach the face, use 1" to 1½" pieces. Apply the hair in the same manner, using 1" to 1½" pieces. Start at the bottom of the head, and work in overlapping rows toward the top.

Mark the eye area lightly with a pencil, and press the black beans into the marks. Place a small dot of hotmelt adhesive in each indentation, and glue the beans in

Adorned with colorful flora, this Santa is a natural complement to your holiday decorations.

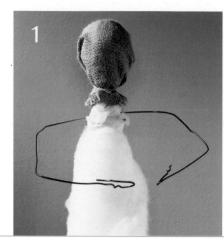

**PHOTO 1:** Center the coat hanger on the front of the batting-wrapped cone below the head, and wrap the wire around the cone. Tape them in place.

**PHOTO 2:** Wrap burlap around the figure, and tie the burlap under the arms.

place. Glue on the red bean for the nose; glue peppergrass leaves below the nose for the mustache. Rub powder blush over the cheek areas.

Cut the sphagnum moss into 1½"-wide strips, and glue the strips around the edges of the sleeves for cuffs. Add lace and green trim to the base of each cuff. Glue clumps of moss to each shoulder and across the back to form the cape. Cut the 3"-wide crocheted lace in half. Gather one edge of each piece with your fingers, and glue the gathers over the shoulders.

Referring to the photo, glue moss, roses, Queen Anne's lace, and pepper berries around the bottom of the robe. Glue maidenhair fern to the burlap front, and add gold trim at the bottom. Let the glue dry.

To make the crown, glue 3" pieces of sweet Annie around the head. Fill in with pepper berries, white and red rosebuds, grapevine tendrils, and broom straws.

Place the figure on the foam-core board, and draw around the outside edges of the robe with a pencil. Cut out the shape, and glue the figure to it with thick white crafts glue. Cover any visible foam-core edges with moss.

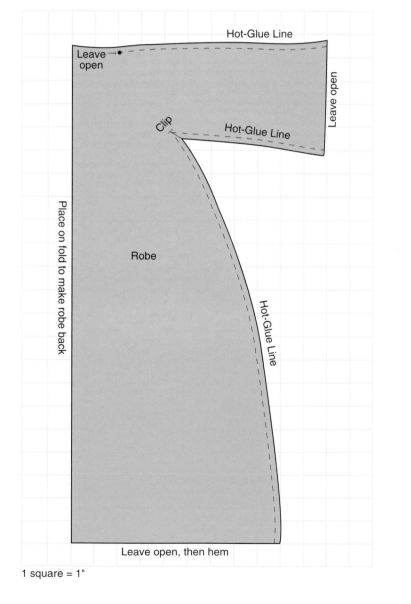

Leave open

Hot-Glue Line

Leave open

Clip

Hot-Glue Line

Place on fold to make robe back

Robe

Hot-Glue Line

Leave open, then hem

1 square = 1"

# NATURE'S FRIEND

Nature lovers will be charmed by this Santa doll made almost entirely from natural materials. Textured earth-tone fabrics, a woolly beard, and an armload of twigs and cones complement the rustic appearance of this woodland wanderer.

# NATURE'S FRIEND

## MATERIALS

- 12"-tall plastic-foam cone (the body)
- Heavy quilt batting: one 11×16" piece, one 1×14" piece
- Tapestry fabric: one 18×20" piece (coat)
- ⅔ yard of cinnamon color felt (the hat, arms, and base)
- Fake fur trim: one 1×45" piece, one ⅝×22" piece
- Brown leather or suede: six 1½×6" pieces, four 1½×9" pieces, two ⅝×10" pieces
- ½ ounce of wool doll hair (the beard)
- ⅜" half-round wooden bead (the nose)
- Acrylic paints: black, flesh color ,tan, and white
- Artist's brushes: small and medium
- Tracing paper

- Assorted seedpods (purchased or found): bell cup (the head), fruit pod (hands), and assorted cattails, acorns, small tree mushrooms, sabulosum, canella, curly protea (hat and bouquet)
- Mini holly and curly willow stems (the bouquet)
- Three 8" to 16"-long purchased pheasant tail feathers (bouquet)
- Small amount of Spanish moss
- Three 1"-long burgundy mushroom birds
- Natural curly raffia (the bow)
- Twelve to sixteen 8"-to 9"-long twigs
- Tracing paper
- Glue gun and hotmelt adhesive
- Hole punch, drill and 1/32" bit, thin wire, needle; heavy-duty thread, scissors

*Santa stands 16" tall. • Designer: Charlene Messerle*

## INSTRUCTIONS
### Assemble the doll

**Body and Arms:** Wrap the plastic-foam cone with an 11×16" piece of quilt batting; secure the batting to the cone by wrapping it with heavy-duty thread. Make the hands by separating the halves of the fruit pod; glue one half to each end of a 16"-long piece of wire. Tightly wrap the wire with a 1×14" piece of batting; secure it to the wire by wrapping it with thread. Cut a 3×14" piece of felt; sew gathering stitches ¼" from each short end. Fold the felt length-wise around the wire; attach it to the wrists by pulling the gathering stitches. Slip-stitch the long felt seam so it lies flat. Sew the center of the arm piece to the center back of the body, 1" below the neck. Secure the arms by tightly wrapping them with thread several times in an X pattern from the back around to the front of the chest; tie the thread tightly.

**Head:** Paint the bell cup seedpod and the wooden bead flesh color. With the opening of the cup at the top, glue the bead to the cup for the nose. Insert a wired stem of purchased bell cup into the top of the body; glue it in place.

### Make the Clothing

To give the fur trim an antique look, dilute 1 part tan paint with 2 parts water. Soak the fur in the diluted paint; squeeze out the excess and let it dry. The fur will look old and matted.

Trace the patterns onto tracing paper; enlarging them as necessary, and cut out. All patterns have ¼" seam allowances.

**Base:** Cut a 20"-diameter circle from the felt. Sew gathering stitches along the outside edges. Set the plastic-foam cone in the center of the circle; pull the threads, pulling the gathered circle up around the cone. Tie off the thread.

**Coat and Bib:** Cut one bib from the cinnamon color felt. Glue the small end of the bib at the neck. Folding the tapestry fabric as shown on the pattern, cut out one coat. With the right sides together; sew the underarm and side seams. Cut the coat along the center line on the front only; machine-zigzag-stitch along all cut edges. Turn the coat right side out.

From the 1"-wide fake fur, cut two 10"-long pieces and one 12"-long piece. Hand-sew a 10"-long piece along each front edge of the coat; sew the 25"-long piece along the coat bottom, mitering the corners. From the ⅝"-wide fake fur, cut two 6"-long pieces; hand-sew them at the sleeve cuffs. Slip the coat over Santa's arms, and slip-stitch at the back of the neck to secure it.

**Hat:** Cut one hat piece from the felt. With the right sides together, sew along the side seam. Turn the hat right side out. Cut a 10"-long piece of ⅝"-wide fake fur, and sew it to the bottom edge of the hat.

**Leather Bag:** Basket-weave the 1½×6" and 1½×9" leather strips into a 6×9" rectangle. Stitch around the outside edges to secure the strips together. Fold the pieced rectangle in half, forming a 4½×6" piece. Use a paper punch to make a hole through both layers near each top corner. To make hanging straps, thread one of the ⅝×10" leather strips through the holes on one side of the bag, knotting the leather inside the bag to hold it in place. Repeat on the other side of the bag. Wrap a bundle of twigs with wire. Place them in the bag, securing the bottom of the sticks to the bag with glue. Hang the bag over the right shoulder; stitch the straps to the coat at the neckline.

### Finish the Doll

Drill a hole in the bottom of each acorn and glue a doubled 8" length of wire into the hole. Gather the seedpods, acorns, cattails, holly, feathers, and curly willow into a pleasing arrangement, and wrap it with wire. Tie a raffia bow, and glue it to the bouquet. Wire the arrangement securely to Santa's left arm.

To make the beard, cut the wool into 3½"-long pieces; glue as much wool as desired around the bottom of the head. To make the hair, cut shorter pieces of wool and glue to the back of the head. Cut a 5" piece for the mustache and glue beneath the nose. Bend the hat to the side, and glue to the head. Glue Spanish moss, tiny tree mushrooms, and two birds to the tip of the hat, and the last bird to the bouquet.

Dip the end of a brush handle into black paint and, with a quick up-and-down motion, make dots for the eyes; add a white dot for a highlight.

**Mother Nature herself provides the most beautiful and bountiful supply of materials *right,* all available for your Santa crafting.**

**HAT**
Cut 1 from felt

**BIB**
Cut 1 from felt

Center line—place on fold
Cut along center line on front only

**COAT FRONT AND BACK**
Cut 1

Shoulder — place on fold

Place lengthwise on grain of fabric

# WOODLAND TRAVELER

## MATERIALS

*Note:* Yardages are based on 45"-wide fabrics.

- ¼ yard of unbleached muslin (the body)
- ⅓ yard of black wool or flannel (the legs)
- ½ yard of dark green corduroy or wool (the pants)
- 22×24" piece of maroon wool, velvet, or flannel (the shirt)
- 16×18" piece of old crazy quilt, wool, or velvet (the vest and hood)
- ⅛ yard or scraps of maroon ribbed-knit cotton fabric (the mittens)
- Two 5×8" scraps of rustic green fabric (the bag)
- Two 2×7" scraps of sherpa fake fur (trim on the boots)
- 1"-wide scraps of real or fake fur (trim on the vest and hood)
- Matching threads; soft-sculpture needle
- 8- to 12-ounce package of wool doll hair or wool roving (the hair)
- A variety of small toys, ornaments, and notions: a canoe, horn, lantern, birdhouse, teddy bear, cloth doll, wood blocks (for the bag)
- A variety of dried or artificial florist's materials: twigs, Spanish moss, pinecones, artificial birds, artificial berries
- 6" artificial Christmas tree
- Fabric paints: black, flesh color, white, and blue, brown, or green for the eyes
- Artist's brushes: Medium round and flat-bristled brush
- Clear satin spray sealer (optional)
- 13" of ⅞"-diameter wood dowel
- 15" log, 4" to 5" inches in diameter
- Drill; woodworker's glue
- Small nails (optional)
- Polyester fiberfill
- Black fine-tip permanent marker
- Powder blush
- 2 yards of jute twine
- 24-gauge wire (optional)
- Glue gun and hotmelt adhesive
- Tracing paper; white chalk pencil

*The doll sits about 16" high.* • *Designer: Tammy Orme*

## INSTRUCTIONS

Trace the patterns onto tracing paper; enlarge if necessary, and cut them out. All stitching is done with right sides together, and all patterns include ¼" seam allowances where needed. Instead of containing hands and arms, the shirt sleeves and mittens are simply stuffed.

### Make the Figure

**Body:** From muslin, cut two bodies. Sew them together, leaving the bottom edge open as marked. Clip the curves, and turn right side out. Turn under the bottom edge ¼" and press.

**Legs:** Fold the black fabric in half with the right sides together. With a white chalk pencil, trace around the leg pattern twice on one side of the black fabric. Leaving the top edge open as marked, sew the layers together with tiny straight stitches, stitching on the traced lines. Cut the pieces out, leaving a narrow seam allowance. Clip the curves; turn right side out; press.

Firmly stuff the head and body to within 1" of the opening. Firmly stuff the bottom 8" of each leg. With the tops of the legs left unstuffed and the toes pointing toward each other, insert the top ¼" of each leg into the opening at the bottom of the body; hand-baste them in place. The Santa should look pigeon-toed at this point; his toes will point in the correct direction after his legs are crossed over the log. Machine-sew across the folded-in edge, closing the body and attaching the legs in one step.

**Nose:** Thread a soft-sculpture needle with thread that matches the fabric; knot one end. Referring to the pattern, insert the needle at A, and give a slight tug on the thread so the knot disappears just under the fabric's surface; catch a small amount of stuffing as you run the needle under the fabric and come up at B. In the same way, insert the needle at C and come up at D. Continuing in this manner, stitch to each letter until you reach J. At J, following the pattern, take several tiny running stitches around the end of the nose; tie and cut the thread. Use the tip of the needle to pull additional stuffing into the nose as needed.

**Face:** With the flat brush, paint the entire face flesh color; let dry. With the round brush, paint the eyeballs white; let the paint dry. Paint irises either blue, green, or brown; let dry. Paint pupils black; let the paint dry. Highlight each pupil with a tiny white dot. When the paint is dry, outline each eye with a black fine-tip permanent marker. Referring to the pattern, draw the eyelids. Color the cheeks and nose with powder blush. If desired, spray everything with a light coat of clear satin sealer.

## Sew the Clothing

**Mittens:** From scraps of knit fabric, cut four mittens. Sew them together in pairs, leaving openings as marked. Turn them right side out; stuff firmly.

**Shirt:** With the 24" edges at the top and bottom, fold the shirt fabric in half from side to side so the fold is on your right. Fold the same piece in half again from top to bottom so the second fold is at the top. Position the shirt pattern on the fabric with the shoulder edge matching the top fold and the center front/back edge matching the right-hand fold. Cut out the shirt. For the neck opening, before unfolding the fabric, cut a 1½"-long slit in both top folds as marked on the pattern.

Open up and refold the fabric so the top and bottom edges meet. Sew the under-

Santa doesn't always travel with eight flying reindeer. This one's been walking through the forest with a canoe on his back in case he needs to cross a woodland stream.

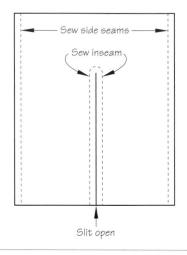

gathering it to fit. Hand-sew the mittens in place. Cut a 1"-wide piece of fur to fit around each wrist. Hot-glue it over the hand stitching.

**Pants:** From corduroy, cut two 9¾×12⅛" pieces. Referring to the diagram *below*, stitch the pieces together at the 12⅛" side seams, and then stitch the inseams; slit them open between the inseams. Clip the corners; turn right side out. Turn under a ¼" hem at the waist and leg openings. Hand-sew the hems in place with gathering stitches. Dress the doll. Pull gathers to fit the doll; secure the threads.

Hot-glue a 2×7" piece of sherpa fake fur around the bottom of each leg to cover the hems. Cut two 24" lengths of jute twine. To tie a boot, place the center of a length of twine on the front of a sherpa cuff about ½" below the top. Bring the ends around to the back; cross the ends in back, and bring them to the front. Cross the ends in front about ½" down from the first wrap and bring to the back; cross the ends in back, and tie them at the center front about ½" down from the second wrap. Tie the second boot in the same way. Trim ties so they're about 1" long.

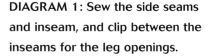

**DIAGRAM 1: Sew the side seams and inseam, and clip between the inseams for the leg openings.**

**Vest and Hood:** From an old crazy quilt or an interesting piece of wool or velvet, cut two hood pieces and one vest. Slit armholes in the vest. For the collar, fold down the corners as marked. If needed, gather the neckline to fit doll.

Sew the top and back seams of hood. Trim excess fabric from point; turn right side out. Insert a small amount of stuffing in the tip. Cut 1"-wide strips of fur to fit around the front of the hood and the outer edges and armholes of the vest; hot-glue in place.

ⓢ **Fill the Woodland Traveler's bag with a small artificial tree and several ornaments and toys.**

arm/side seams. Hem the bottom edge. Clip the inside corners; turn the shirt right side out. Turn under the neck opening ¼"; hand-sew running stitches around the neck ⅛" from the folded edge. Fold under the wrist ends of the sleeves ¼". Hand-sew gathering stitches ⅛" in from the folded edges. Put the shirt on the doll. Pull the thread at the neckline, gathering it to fit; tie off the thread.

For the arms, lightly stuff each sleeve. Insert the top edge of one mitten into each wrist and pull the thread on the sleeves,

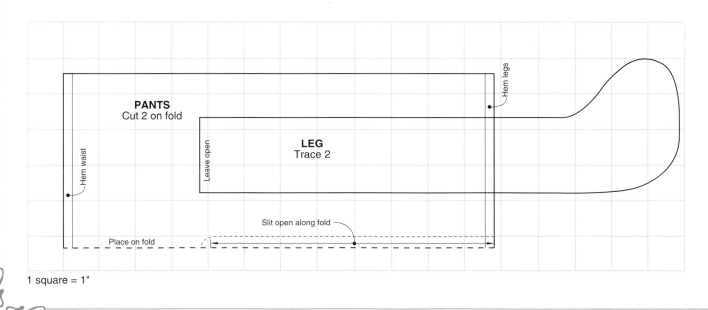

1 square = 1"

Place the vest and the hood on the doll and hot-glue the hood.

**Bag:** Sew together two 5×8" pieces of fabric, leaving one 5" end open. Turn right side out. Fill half of the bag with stuffing. Hot-glue a small artificial tree in back. Glue several ornaments and toys in front of the tree. About 1½" down from the top of the bag, tie the remaining ½ yard of jute twine.

## Assemble the Santa

Place the log on its flattest side. On top of the log, about 7" in from one end, drill a ⅞"-diameter hole 3" to 4" deep. Squirt some woodworker's glue in the hole. Insert the dowel, and let the glue dry.

Lifting up Santa's vest and shirt, cut a small slit in the back of the muslin body. Apply hot glue to the exposed end of the dowel. Referring to the photo for placement, quickly pull Santa over the dowel so he sits on the log at a slight angle. Pull down and arrange his clothing, gluing it to the dowel as needed so he sits securely. If needed, secure him to the dowel by wrapping wire around his waist.

Hot-glue the bag to the log. Hang a toy or ornament over one arm, and bend the arm upward so it looks as though he's holding the bag. Hot-glue the arm in place. Fill in empty spots with pinecones, artificial berries, and Spanish moss.

Referring to the photo, cross Santa's legs. Glue or nail them in place. Hang a toy or ornament on the other arm. Curve the arm in front of the chest so he can carry more items; hot-glue it in place. Hot-glue twigs and toys to his arm.

**Hair and Beard:** Separate and fluff the wool. For eyebrows, glue a tiny length of wool above each eye. Hot-glue the wool around Santa's face, varying the lengths for a natural look.

For the mustache, cut an 8"-long piece of wool. Tightly wrap the center of this piece with matching thread; knot the thread. Center the mustache horizontally just below the nose and hot-glue it in place. Trim the hair as needed.

Hot-glue a tiny nest of Spanish moss on top of Santa's hat. Add a small artificial bird and some berries to the nest. If desired, shape a pair of glasses from 24-gauge wire; glue them to Santa's face.

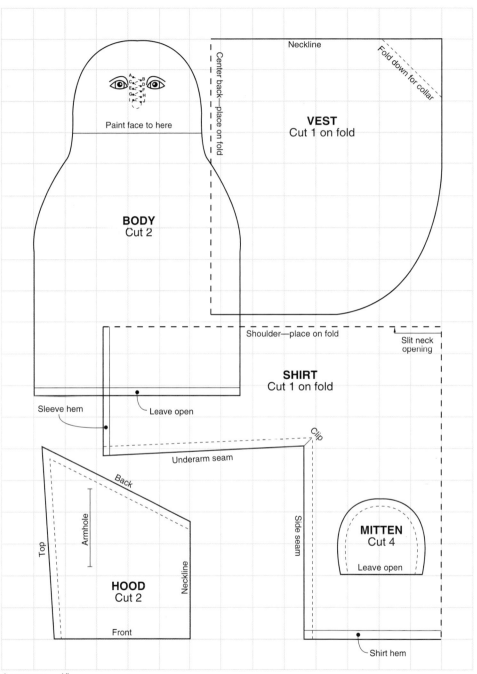

1 square = 1"

Rich fabrics, glistening trims, and a white feather boa, make this Stately Old Gent an elegant addition to your Christmas decor.

# A STATELY OLD GENT

## MATERIALS

### Paper-Clay Head
- Paper clay
- 1½" plastic-foam egg
- Old stiff-bristle paintbrush
- Flat toothpick; sharp pencil
- Acrylic crafts paints: country red, dusty peach, medium blue
- Artist's synthetic paintbrushes
- Matte acrylic sealer

### Body
- 1" pine: one 3×2½" and one 3×10½" piece
- Wire coat hanger; wire cutter; needle-nose pliers
- Drill bit to make a snug hole for the wire
- Woodworker's glue
- Two 1¼" brads; hammer

### Clothing
- ½ yard of red satin (the undergarment)
- ½ yard of ivory wool (the coat)
- ½ yard of ivory lining (the coat)
- ¾ yard of metallic gold cording (the belt)
- Small piece of white fabric for the mittens
- 1½ yards of ⅝"-wide white/gold embroidered ribbon
- ¾ yard of ⅜"-wide metallic ribbon
- Blue metallic seed beads (optional)
- ¼" brass jingle bell
- ⅓ yard of white feather boa with metallic threads
- Polyester fiberfill
- Gold glitter spray
- Crafts glue; glue gun and hotmelt adhesive
- Fray Check seam sealant
- Curly white wool doll hair
- 11mm-diameter traditional brass curtain rod
- Holly leaf and berry

*Doll sits about 15¹/₂" high.  •  Designer: Brenda Terry*

## INSTRUCTIONS

### Sculpt Head and Shoulders

**Note:** Before sculpting the head, practice the following exercises to learn how to "mend" paper clay.

Mending refers to using the tips of the brush bristles, water, and a gentle yet aggressive scrubbing motion to join two pieces of clay.

**Exercise 1:** Wet a dime-size piece of clay, and dab and scrub the tips of an old bristle brush against it until a thick slime, called slip, forms.

**Exercise 2:** Roll two balls of clay, one the size of a pea and the other three times larger. Flatten each ball to ¼". Moisten one side of each circle, and place the wet surfaces together. Mend the edges of a smaller circle to a larger surface. Brush the slip off the surface of the clay. Repeat until all crevices are gone.

**Head:** Roll out a portion of paper clay to ¼" thick. Cover the plastic-foam egg with rolled-out clay, mending the seams together. Remove the excess clay. The narrow end of the egg is the bottom of the head.

**Nose:** Roll a narrow ½"-long tube of clay. Mend the clay to the center of the head for a nose. Press around the tube edges with the end of a paintbrush, narrowing the width of the nose at the top. Pinch the tip of the nose into shape. Use a toothpick to indent the nostrils. Smooth the surface, using a paintbrush and water.

**Mouth:** Use the point of a pencil to make a hole ⅛" under the nose so the mouth appears to be whistling. Gently press underneath the bottom edge of the mouth with the flat end of a toothpick to form the lower lip. Smooth the mouth, using the brush and water.

**Eyelids:** Roll two balls of clay half the size of peas, and flatten them a bit. Position and mend the balls to the face, so the eyes appear to be closed. Use the end of a paintbrush to press the top edge of each eyelid even with the forehead. Smooth the eyelids, using the brush and water.

**Cheeks:** Roll two balls of clay the size of peas, and flatten them a bit. Position them on the face just below the eyelids, and mend them to the face. Use the end of a paintbrush to press the edges of the cheeks even with the face. Smooth the cheeks, using the brush and water.

**Neck and Shoulders:** Using a portion of clay the size of Santa's head, form the neck and shoulders; they should measure 3"× ¾", resembling the figure, *below*.

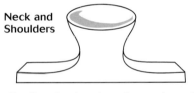

Neck and Shoulders

Position the head on the neck so the head is angled upward; mend it in place. Allow the clay to dry according to the manufacturer's instructions.

**Painting:** Paint the head, neck, and shoulders with dusty peach. Paint the mouth country red. Lightly dry-brush country red between the cheeks and nose and underneath the cheeks; lightly brush over the eyelids as well. Use a wash of medium blue to underline the eyelids. After the paint is dry, apply matte acrylic sealer.

### Form the Body

Using woodworker's glue and two brads, glue and nail the 3×10½" body piece of pine upright to the flat 3×2½" base piece, evenly spacing the nails at the bottom of the base. Set the nails.

Using a bit that will provide a snug fit for the wire, drill holes ¼" below the top edge

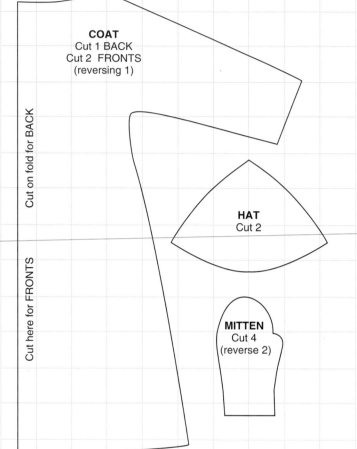

**COAT**
Cut 1 BACK
Cut 2 FRONTS
(reversing 1)

Cut on fold for BACK

Cut here for FRONTS

**HAT**
Cut 2

**MITTEN**
Cut 4
(reverse 2)

1 Square = 1 Inch

on each ¾" side. Cut two 8" lengths of wire. Insert the wires into the holes. Measure and cut the wires 7" from the wood. Gently remove the wires. Using needle-nose pliers, bend back ¼" at one end of each wire, forming a tiny loop. Next, bend back ¾" to form the hand.

Glue the paper-clay shoulders to the top edge of the body piece. For a smooth transition, mend the shoulders to the wood with additional clay and slip.

## Make the Clothes

Enlarge the patterns onto tracing paper; cut them out. All patterns include ¼" seam allowances. All stitching is done with the right sides together. Clip the curves and press the seams.

**Undergarment:** Cut a 15×18" piece of red satin; stitch together the 15" edges for the back seam.

Sew gathering stitches along the 18" top and bottom edges. Place the garment on the doll body, and pull the gathering threads to fit around the shoulders (but not pulled up tight around the neck), and around the bottom edges of a 3×10½" piece of wood. Secure gathering threads.

Adjust the fabric at the bottom so it puffs out over the wood base. Reinsert the wire arms into the holes, piercing the fabric. Tie gold cording around the waist; trim the ends to the desired length.

**Coat:** Cut the wool and lining pieces. Sew the fronts to the backs along the top edges

of the sleeves and the underarm and side seams. Turn the wool coat right side out. Place the wool and lining coats with the right sides together, and sew around the front edges and hem. Turn the coat right side out; press.

The sleeve edges will remain raw until the arms have been positioned. Topstitch the embroidered ribbon along the front and hem edges, mitering the corners. If desired, glue seed beads to the ribbon. Spray the coat with gold glitter and set it aside.

**Hat:** Cut the hat pieces. Sew the pieces together, leaving the bottom edge open. Turn to the right side; press.

Baste under the raw edge ½". Stitch the embroidered ribbon around the hat edge. Glue seed beads to the ribbon (optional). Stitch the bell to the point of the hat. Spray the hat with gold glitter, and set it aside.

**Mittens:** Cut the mitten pieces. Stitch them together in pairs, leaving the straight edges open; turn.

Sew gathering stitches around the open end of the mittens. Stuff the mittens with fiberfill, and place them on the wire arms, pushing the wire ends into the stuffing to within ¼" of the fingertip area. Pull the gathering threads tight, and secure them by winding them around the "wrist." Apply hotmelt adhesive over the mitten ends to secure the mittens to the wire. Spray the mittens with gold glitter.

**Finish:** Place the coat on the body. Tack the front opening closed at the neck edge. Bend the arms. Turn the sleeve edges under to the appropriate length.

Apply seam sealant to the ends of the feather boa. Place the boa around the neck edge of the coat and secure with a few invisible stitches. Glue the hair, beard, and mustache to the head. Glue the hat on the head.

Cut a 16" length of a traditional brass curtain rod; position and hot-glue it in Santa's hand. Tie ⅜"-wide metallic ribbon around the rod, making a bow. Hot-glue a few holly leaves and a berry to the bow.

# GOSH, IT'S GOURDS

Designer: Dee Robinson

Big or little, short or tall—any gourd is the perfect
shape for a painted, *right,* or woodburned, *left,*
Santa face adapted from these patterns.

# PAINTED GOURD SANTA

## MATERIALS

- Dried gourd with a flat bottom that measures about 26" long and 22" around at the widest point
- ½ yard of unbleached muslin (beard)
- 4×18" piece of fur or short-nap artificial fur
- Three 1×18" wool strips (the braid)
- Acrylic paints: black, blue, country red, light tan, off-white, peach, and dark pink
- Assorted artist's brushes, including a liner brush
- Palette knife
- Acrylic modeling paste
- Dark brown antiquing medium
- Matte finish spray sealer
- Tea bags (to stain the muslin)
- Two ½" bells
- Twelve 24" lengths of jute twine
- Artificial red and gold berries
- Tracing paper; graphite paper
- Fine-grit sandpaper
- Glue gun and hotmelt adhesive
- Wooden beads (as needed to level the gourd)

## INSTRUCTIONS

To clean the gourd, refer to the instructions for the Woodburned Gourd Santa, *opposite.* Lightly sand the gourd smooth with fine-grit sandpaper; wipe off any sanding dust before beginning to paint.

### Paint the Gourd

Paint the gourd with two coats of country red. Enlarge the pattern *right,* if necessary, to fit your gourd; trace the pattern onto tracing paper. When the country red paint is dry, use graphite paper to transfer the outline of the face to the gourd. Paint the face peach; let the paint dry. Transfer all facial details onto the gourd.

Paint the eyes off-white and the upper eyelids light tan. Paint a blue circle inside each eye for irises; paint a smaller black circle in each blue circle for pupils. Referring to the pattern, paint each iris with fine off-white lines. Paint eyelashes with fine black lines; outline the eyes and nose and paint nostrils with black, using a liner brush. Paint the inside of the mouth and outline the lower lip with black.

To highlight the eyes, dip the tip of a liner brush handle into off-white and paint it with a dot in each pupil. To highlight the tip of the nose, paint with a wash of dark pink. Add the thin light tan comma stroke on the right side of tip of the nose. Apply a wash of dark pink down center of nose and under eyes for cheeks; highlight cheeks with light tan comma strokes. Paint the lower lip dark pink. Highlight the right side of the lower lip with a light tan comma stroke. Let the paint dry.

For the eyebrows, apply a thin layer of modeling paste with a palette knife. For the

mustache, apply a ¹⁄₁₆ to ⅛" layer of modeling paste. When the modeling paste is dry enough to hold its shape, swirl the tip of the palette knife through the paste to add texture to the mustache. Clean the palette knife immediately. Let the modeling paste dry for several hours.

Following the manufacturer's instructions, apply antiquing medium to the entire gourd. When the medium is dry, spray the gourd with a light coat of sealer; let it dry, then apply another coat.

### Make the Beard

Cut two 10×16" pieces of muslin. Place one piece on top of the other and fold it in half to make a 5×16" piece. Sew ⅛" from the fold through all four layers of fabric. To make the fringe, cut from the open 16" edge to the stitched line, cutting every ¼" through all layers and taking care not to cut the stitching.

Use tea bags to make a strong solution of hot tea. Soak the fringed muslin in tea.

Squeeze out excess moisture, and dry the fabric in a clothes dryer on the hot setting. When the fabric is dry, the beard will look stringy. Untangle the beard, leaving most loose threads attached. With the fringe facing upward, and covering Santa's face, glue the stitched edge around the face below the mustache. Hold the beard in place until the glue dries. Let the fringe fall into place; trim the beard, if necessary.

### Add the Fur and Trim

Fold the fur lengthwise so the raw edges meet in the center; glue it in place. With the raw edges down, glue the fur around the top of the face. To make the trim, braid three 1×18" wool strips; secure the ends with glue. Fold the braid in half, and glue the center to the bottom left edge of the fur strip. Align the jute twine pieces and treat them as one; tie them into a bow and glue to the braid. Glue berries to the jute twine bow. Glue bells to the ends of the braid. Level the gourd by gluing wooden beads to the base.

# WOODBURNED GOURD SANTA

## MATERIALS

- One 12"-long dried gourd with a flat bottom and a crooked neck
- Wood burning tool
- Acrylic paints: black, blue, green, light tan, off-white, and red
- Assorted artist's brushes, including a fine liner
- Dark brown antiquing medium
- Matte-finish acrylic spray sealer
- 1½×10" strip of wool
- Tracing paper; graphite paper
- Abrasive sponge; abrasive household cleanser
- Glue gun and hotmelt adhesive
- Wooden beads (as needed to level the gourd)

## INSTRUCTIONS

Soak the dried gourd in hot soapy water for a few minutes. Scrape the gourd with an abrasive sponge to remove large discolored spots, and then scrub the gourd with the sponge and abrasive cleanser. Rinse well and let dry overnight. The gourd will dry to its natural light brown color.

Enlarge the face patterns, if necessary, and trace them onto tracing paper. Use graphite paper to transfer the pattern for the face and as many holly leaves as desired onto the gourd. Using the wood-burning tool, burn along all lines, using slow, firm strokes to make deep, smooth lines. When the burning is complete, wipe off any residue with a soft cloth.

Referring to the patterns, paint the holly leaves green. Paint the berries red. Paint the mustache off-white. Paint each eye off-white and each upper eyelid light tan. Paint a blue circle inside each eye for irises; paint a smaller black circle in each blue circle for pupils. Paint each iris with fine off-white lines; paint eyelashes with fine black lines. To highlight the eyes, dip the tip of a liner brush handle into off-white, and paint a dot in each pupil.

Using the wood-burning tool, outline the eyes, nose, eyebrows, and mustache again. Using a fine liner brush, lightly paint along all burned lines with black, wiping off the excess paint before it dries. Make a thin wash of dark pink by mixing red with off-white and water. Apply the dark pink wash to the tip of the nose and under the eyes for cheeks; add highlights of off-white to the cheeks as shown on the pattern. Paint a light-tan comma stroke on the right side of the tip of the nose. Let it dry.

Brush antiquing medium on the gourd, wiping off any excess but leaving a little around the mustache as an accent. Let the medium dry. Spray the gourd with sealer.

Tie the strip of wool into a bow. Glue the bow to the top or tip of the gourd. Check to see if the gourd sits flat. Level it by gluing wooden beads to the base as needed.

# SANTA DOLL

*The Santa doll is 18" tall • Designer: Betty Auth*

## MATERIALS

### For the Face and Body

- Santa face push mold
- 1 ounce of polymer clay: flesh color
- Two pale-blue seed beads (the eyes)
- Baby powder; powder blush
- Wool doll hair or roving
- 18" muslin doll body
- 18" piece of 20-gauge wire (the arms)
- Two 12"-long pieces of ⅛" dowel
- 5" doll needle; sewing needle
- Ivory carpet thread
- Scissors; ruler; pencil
- Tracing paper
- Tacky crafts glue
- Needle-nose pliers; crafts knife
- Knitting needle or toothpick
- Aluminum foil

*Note:* Adjust your yardages if your doll is a different size.

### For the Clothing

- 4×6" piece of mat board (the boot soles)
- Two 2×7" pieces of high-loft quilt batting (the boots)
- One pair of white newborn size baby socks
- Ivory flannel: two 10×13½" pieces (the coat base), one 5¼×12" piece (the bag base)
- White brocade or Jacquard: two 9×10" pieces (the pants), two 5½×6" pieces (the sleeves)
- Ivory or white textured fabric: one 5×11" piece (the shirt),

four 2½×4" pieces (the mittens), one 8×10" piece (the cap)
- White tulle netting with gold glitter: two 6×9" pieces (the oversleeves)
- 2 yards of 1½"-wide sheer metallic gold ribbon (the boots)
- 1¼"-wide ivory satin ribbon: 12" piece (the binding for bag), two 8" pieces (the binding for coat armholes)
- ¼ yard each of 8–10 different white and ivory holiday ribbons (the coat and bag crazy quilting)
- Brown plush ⅞" felt: two 1½×5½" pieces (the sleeve cuffs), two 1×5½" pieces (the boot cuffs), two 1×13" pieces (the front edges of the coat), one 1×4¾" piece (shoulder of the coat)
- Polyester fiberfill (the cap and the bag)
- Sewing thread: gold and ivory

### For the Trimmings

- 18" piece of 1"-wide gold fringe (the coat bottom)
- 45" piece of ¼"-wide metallic gold pre-gathered ribbon (cap, sleeves, and bag)
- 22" length of metallic gold stretch cord (the bag strap)
- Two 4"-long ivory tassels (the cap and bag)
- Twelve ¼"-diameter metallic gold ribbon roses (the bag tassel)
- Pearl glass seed beads (the tassels)
- Small gold beads (the cap tassel)
- White cake-decorating dove
- Ivory artificial berries with leaves
- Dried green moss

## ESSENCE OF ELEGANCE

## INSTRUCTIONS

### Make the Doll

**Face:** Dust the inside of the mold with baby powder; shake out the excess. Form the polymer clay into a ball, and roll it into a teardrop shape. Place the point of the teardrop shape into the nose of the mold, and push down firmly with your thumb to fill the mold. Extend the clay down about ½" to form a neck that is at least ¼" thick. Carefully remove the clay from the mold.

With a knitting needle or toothpick, pierce six holes around the outside edge of the face where they'll be covered by the beard and hair. These holes will be used to join the face to the doll head. Deepen the wrinkles in the clay face and make nostrils with the knitting needle. Place a pale-blue seed bead on the tip of the knitting needle, and push it straight into the center of each eye. Mold each upper eyelid with the knitting needle so it slightly covers the bead. Manipulate the clay into the desired facial expression, referring to the photo on *page 140, top right*. Brush powder blush over the cheeks and the tip of the nose. Place the face on a doubled sheet of aluminum foil, and bake in a 265° oven for 30 minutes.

Thread a doll needle with a 24" length of carpet thread; knot the ends. Starting and ending at the back of the muslin doll head, firmly sew the face to the head through the holes. Tie the threads at the back of the head.

**Legs:** Sharpen one end of each dowel with a crafts knife. Insert the sharpened end of one dowel into one muslin doll heel, and push it up through the leg, exiting at the top of the leg and entering again in the doll body; keep pushing until the bottom of the dowel is 2" above the foot. Repeat for the other side.

**Arms:** Cut a piece of wire 1" shorter than the outstretched muslin arms. Insert the wire into one hand, and thread the wire through the arm, across the shoulders, and through the other arm until both ends are hidden inside the arms.

## Make the Clothes

All clothing is sewn using ¼" seam allowances unless otherwise specified. Trace the patterns onto tracing paper, enlarging them as necessary, and cut them out.

**Boots:** Trace patterns for the innersole and the outer sole twice onto mat board; cut them out with a crafts knife. Cut two outer soles from sheer metallic gold ribbon and glue one to the bottom of each mat-board outer sole; set them aside.

Referring to Diagram 1, *below*, glue one mat-board innersole to the bottom of each muslin foot. To hold each sole in place, wrap the foot and inner sole with carpet thread without compressing the foot. Fold

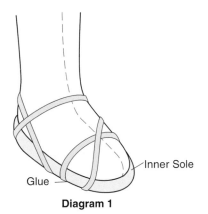

Glue

Inner Sole

**Diagram 1**

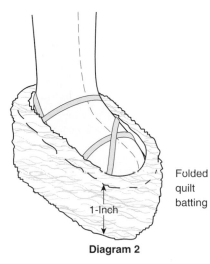

Folded quilt batting

1-Inch

**Diagram 2**

Strolling through a starry winter wonderland, this Elegant Santa is a romantic fantasy of a doll. With his ribboned-decked robes and richly textured clothing, he looks like a one-of-a-kind designer doll. Not so! His body is ready-made and his expressive face is made in a mold.

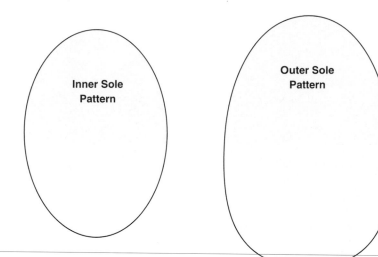

**Inner Sole Pattern**

**Outer Sole Pattern**

**Mitten Pattern**

Glass beads pressed into the eye area will give your Santa a realistic expression.

Wrap boots with ribbons to construct Santa's laces.

a 2×7" strip of quilt batting in half lengthwise. Referring to Diagram 2, *page 139*, wrap the strip around the outside of one foot with the edge of the batting even with the sole, beginning and ending at the heel; glue it in place. Repeat for the other foot. Put a sock on each foot, pulling the sock up to the knee; stitch in place.

Cut the remaining sheer metallic gold ribbon in half to make two 33"-long pieces. Thread a sewing needle with gold sewing thread, knotting one end. To make a boot, refer to the photograph, at *right,* and wrap ribbon around the foot. Begin wrapping at the heel, tacking the ribbon in place and ending under the foot to hide the raw edge. Repeat for the other boot. Spread glue on the uncovered sides of the outer soles, and position the soles on the bottoms of the boots so Santa can stand alone; let the glue dry.

**Mittens:** Pin together 2½×4" pieces of textured fabric in pairs with the right sides together. Trace the mitten pattern onto each set with a pencil; do not cut them out. With a sewing machine set on the short stitch, sew on the traced lines; cut the mittens out, allowing for ⅛" seam allowances; turn right side out. Pull the mittens over the hands, and hand-sew them to the hands around the top edges.

**Shirt:** Referring to Diagram 3, *opposite*, fold a 5×11" piece of textured fabric in

half, forming a 5×5½" rectangle. Cut a slit from the center of one raw edge to the fold as shown on Diagram 3. Cut a slit along the fold 1" toward each shoulder as shown. Place the shirt on the body with the slit at the back, tuck under the raw edges, and tack the shirt to the body.

To make a sleeve, fold one 5½×6" piece of brocade with the right sides together, forming a 5½×3" rectangle; sew along the 5½" edge to make the underarm seam. Press the seam allowances open, and turn right side out. Turn under the raw edge of the sleeve at the shoulder and sew it with a gathering stitch. Place it on the doll, and pull the thread tightly to fit

around the shoulder; sew the sleeve to the body. Repeat for the other sleeve.

To make an oversleeve, fold a 6×9" piece of tulle with the right sides together, forming a 6×4½" rectangle; sew along the 6" edge to make the underarm seam. Turn right side out. Turn under the raw edge at the shoulder and sew it with a gathering stitch. Place the oversleeve over the shirt sleeve, and pull the thread tightly to fit at the shoulder; sew the oversleeve to the shirt. Sew the gathering stitches around the open end of the oversleeve; pull the thread so the oversleeve fits the sleeve; tack it to the sleeve with the raw edge of the oversleeve about ¼" closer to the shoulder than to the raw edge of the sleeve. The oversleeve should pouf out from the sleeve. Fold a 1½×5½" felt cuff in half lengthwise, and hand-sew to bind the raw edges of the sleeve and oversleeve. Repeat for the other oversleeve.

**Pants:** Referring to Diagram 4, *below,* sew together the two 9×10" pieces of brocade along the 10" sides with the right sides together. Find the center of one 9" side, and mark a line extending 5" into the fabric. Stitch ¼" around the marked line to form the inseam; cut on the marked line. Turn the waist and the bottoms of the pant legs under ¼"; press. Put the pants on the doll, and hand-sew gathering stitches at the bottom of the pant legs and at the waist; pull the threads to fit, and tack the pants to the doll. Glue a 1×5½" strip of felt over the bottom of one pant leg and the top of the boot; repeat for the other side.

**Cap:** Fold an 8×10" piece of textured fabric in half with the right sides together, forming a 4×10" piece; sew along the long edge to form a tube. Turn right side out; turn under the raw edges and finger

crease. Sew gathering stitches around one end; pull the thread tightly. Referring to Diagram 6, *page 142,* trim one tassel by gluing small gold beads to the top; sew the tassel to the gathered end of the cap.

## Make the Coat and Bag
The coat and bag are cut from crazy-quilt-style fabric made of ribbons sewn on a base of flannel. After the ribbons are cut, sew the ribbons to the base fabric. Using any combination of ribbon widths, pin ribbons randomly to the base fabric, sometimes overlapping each other. Cover the base fabric completely (see Diagram 5, *below*). Machine-sew all ribbons to the base close to their edges. Sew around the outside edges of the base fabric, and trim the ribbon ends that extend over the edges of the base.

**Bag:** Cover a 5¼×12" piece of ivory flannel with ribbons as described above. Fold the fabric with the right sides together to form a 5¼×6" piece; stitch along both 6" edges and turn right side out. Fold a 12" length of 1¼" satin ribbon in half lengthwise, and finger-crease; cut the ribbon to fit around the top of the bag, allowing for a ½" overlap. Hand-sew the ribbon to the bag,

binding the raw edges; tuck under the overlapping end. Sew a length of ¼" metallic gold pregathered ribbon beneath the ribbon binding. Embellish the remaining 4"-long tassel by sewing or gluing pearl glass seed beads and metallic gold ribbon roses to cover the top. Sew the tassel to the front of the bag. Coil ¼" metallic gold ribbon into a rosette; glue it above the tassel. Sew one end of a 22" length of gold stretch cord to each side of the bag to make a strap.

**Coat:** Cut two 10×13½" pieces of flannel on the trim lines as shown in Diagram 7, *page 142.* Sew together the pieces along the 10" edge with the right sides together. Press the seam allowances open. Cover the coat base with ribbons as described above and trim the excess ribbon. Pin a 1×13" felt strip to each center front edge of the coat with the right side of the felt strip to the wrong side of the coat. Fold the felt around the edge to the front; glue or sew it to the coat front to hold it in place. Place a 1×4¾" felt strip over the shoulder seam, and sew along both edges to hide the shoulder seam.

Fold an 8" strip of 1¼" satin ribbon in half crosswise; finger-crease it. Fold it

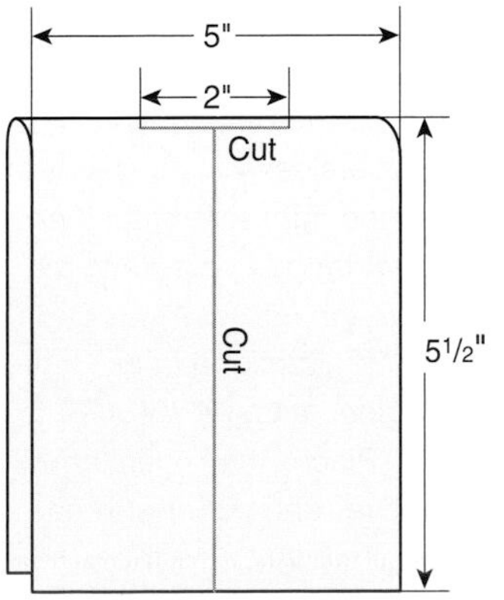

**Diagram 3 – Shirt**

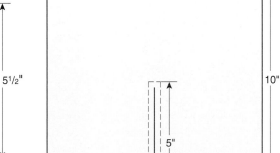
**Diagram 4 – Pants**

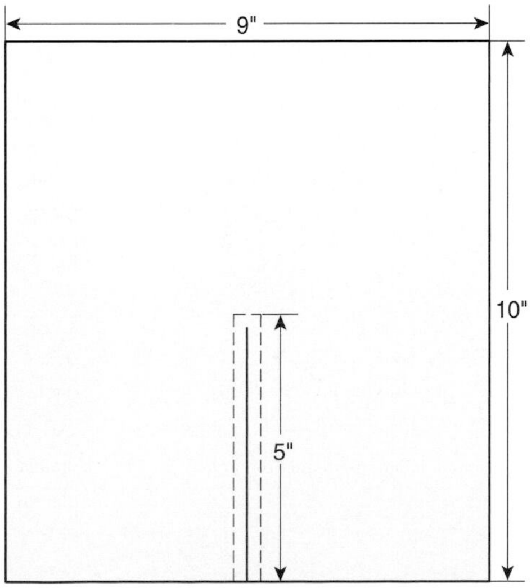

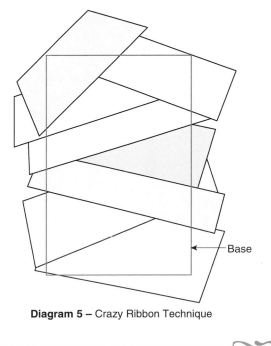
**Diagram 5 – Crazy Ribbon Technique**

again lengthwise; press. Align the center of the ribbon with the shoulder seam, and sew the ribbon to the coat as a binding for the coat sleeve edge (see Diagram 8, *below*). Repeat for the other side. Fold the coat with the right sides together, and sew the side seams, ending about ½" past the raw edges of the ribbon; press the seam allowances to one side, and topstitch along the raw edge to hold it flat. Sew or glue the fringe around the coat hem.

## Finish the Doll

Pull curly wool gently until it separates into pieces with soft feathery edges.

For the eyebrows, glue tiny matching pieces of wool above the eyes. For the beard, apply glue in a semicircle to frame the bottom of the face from ear to ear; apply bits of wool to cover the chin. For the hair, apply glue to the back of the head and above the forehead; cover it with wool. Trim the beard and hair to the desired length.

For the mustache, pull off a thin 5"-long strand of wool; moisten your fingertips, and twist each end to a point. Twist the strand in the center, and glue it beneath the nose, covering the upper lip. Glue a small mound of polyester fiberfill to the crown of the head.

**Trimmings:** Place the thin line of glue above each sleeve cuff, and glue on small lengths of gold pregathered ribbon. Apply a line of glue on the inside edge of the cap, and pull over polyester fiberfill on the head, with the seam at one side; let the glue dry. Place a line of glue around the bottom edge of the cap, and trim with two rows of

gold pregathered ribbon. Sew a 4"-long piece of ribbon at the pants waist for the belt. Stuff the bag with a small amount of polyester fiberfill; arrange the moss and artificial berries with leaves on top of the fiberfill; glue them in place. Glue a cake-decorating dove to one of Santa's hands. Bend the arm wires to pose the doll.

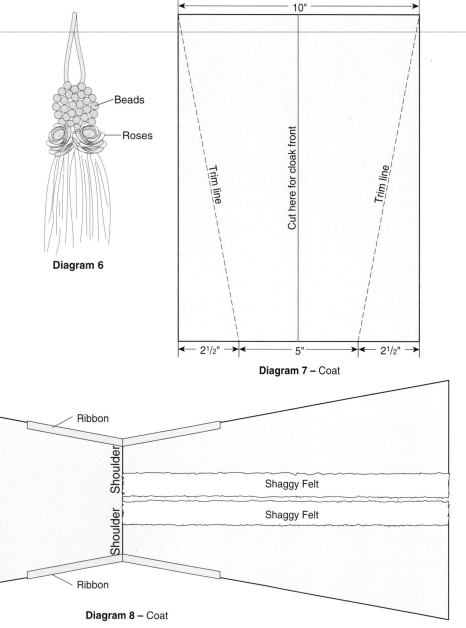

Beads

Roses

**Diagram 6**

10"

Trim line

Cut here for cloak front

Trim line

2½"   5"   2½"

**Diagram 7** – Coat

Ribbon

Shoulder

Shoulder

Shaggy Felt

Shaggy Felt

Ribbon

**Diagram 8** – Coat

*Box is about 5x7½" • Designer: Susan Cousineau*

# PAPIER-MÂCHÉ BOX

## MATERIALS
- Basic Santa Face (see *page 145*)
- One 5×7½" oval papier-mâché box
- Matte acrylic spray sealer
- 18"-long piece of cotton lace trim
- Acrylic paint: metallic gold
- Fabric stiffener
- Water-based antiquing gel
- 1"-wide paintbrush
- Spray glitter: gold
- Artificial evergreen sprig and red berry
- Glue gun and hotmelt adhesive

## INSTRUCTIONS

Spray the papier-mâché box with acrylic sealer for a smooth, nonporous surface; let the sealer dry. Use a 1"-wide brush to paint all box surfaces metallic gold; let the paint dry. Dip the cotton lace trim into fabric stiffener, and position it around the edges of the box top; let the stiffener dry.

Make a wash with 4 parts water and 1 part antiquing glaze. Brush the wash on the outside of the box; let the glaze dry. Spray gold glitter on the box; let the glitter dry. Spray the box with acrylic sealer; let the sealer dry. Hot-glue the Santa face to the box top.

Pull the curly wool apart to fluff it. Run a thin line of hotmelt adhesive around the face, and attach the wool as desired for the hair and beard. Roll two small pieces of wool between your fingers to make a mustache; hot-glue it beneath the nose. Hot-glue the evergreen sprig and berry at one side of the hair.

## MATERIALS

### For Each Ornament

- Basic Santa Face with beard and hair (See the instructions opposite)
- Crib-size cotton batting (to make several ornaments)
- 30×45" piece of fusible web
- Crocheted doilies (For the number and shape, see individual ornaments below.)
- 12–24 tea bags
- Fabric stiffener
- Water-based antiquing gel
- Spray glitter: gold
- Acrylic spray sealer
- Glue gun and hotmelt adhesive
- Small nail or pushpin
- Florist's wire (For lengths, see individual ornaments below.)
- ½" dowel or wooden spoon
- Natural raffia
- Tracing paper; marking pen
- Waxed paper
- Scissors; pinking shears
- Paper towels

### For Each Candy Cane

- One finished candy-cane-shape ornament
- One 3½" round crocheted doily with scalloped edges
- 27" length of florist's wire
- Gold bead garland: one 3¼" length, two 2" lengths
- Trimmings: artificial evergreen sprig and berry and 13mm gold bell

### For Each Star

- One finished star-shape ornament
- One 3½" round crocheted doily with scalloped edges
- 33" length of florist's wire
- One 1" wooden star
- Trimmings: Artificial evergreen sprig and red berry, one pearl button, two 6 mm gold bells
- Acrylic paint: metallic gold

# VICTORIAN SANTA ORNAMENTS

## INSTRUCTIONS

*Following the instructions opposite, make one Basic Santa Face for each ornament you plan to make.*

### Make the Basic Ornaments

Soak tea bags in boiling water to make a tea-dye solution. Tea-dye the cotton batting and doilies or lace trim by soaking them until they reach the desired color. Dry them on waxed paper.

Cut the crib-size batting in half crosswise. Fuse the batting pieces together, following the manufacturer's instructions for the fusible webbing.

Enlarge the patterns on the grid and cut them out. Pin the patterns on the fused batting, and trace the shapes with a marking pen. Cut them out with pinking shears.

Following the manufacturer's instructions for the fabric stiffener, apply the stiffener to the cotton-batting shapes. Let the shapes dry on waxed paper, turning them frequently for speed drying. Make a wash of 4 parts water and 1 part antiquing glaze; brush the wash on each shape. Blot the excess glaze with paper towel; let the glaze dry. Dip a doily into fabric stiffener, and apply it to each individual ornament. Spray the ornament with gold glitter and let dry. Spray with sealer.

To attach hanging wires, use a small nail or pushpin to make holes in the ornaments. Cut a length of wire as indicated for each ornament. Coil the wire around a dowel or wooden spoon handle; remove the dowel or spoon. Following the instructions for each individual ornament, thread each end of the wire through a hole; twist the ends around the hanging wire to secure them. Using raffia, tie a bow around the top of the coiled wire; secure it with hotmelt adhesive.

### Trim the Ornaments

**Candy Cane:** Cut the edges from a scalloped doily. Cut one length with three scallops and two lengths with two scallops each. Apply fabric stiffener to the pieces of trim, and place them on the candy cane to form stripes, with the scalloped edges toward the bottom; let the stiffener dry. Spray glitter on the candy cane, evergreen sprig, and berry; let the glitter dry. Glue a piece of bead garland to the upper edge of each piece of scalloped trim. Glue the Santa face to the candy cane with the top of the face even with the inside curve of the candy cane. Glue the beard and hair to the face. Glue

# BASIC SANTA FACE

## MATERIALS
- Paper clay
- Acrylic paint: black, flesh, gray, ivory, red
- Assorted artist's paintbrushes, including a liner
- Water-based antiquing gel
- Matte acrylic spray sealer
- White curly wool (the hair and beard)
- Glue gun and hotmelt adhesive
- Waxed paper
- Toothpick

## INSTRUCTIONS
**Note:** *Refer to the photographs of finished projects shown on pages 143-145 for Santa face details. Cover your work surface with waxed paper. Mix the paper clay according to manufacturer's instructions.*

### Mold the Face
Form a 1" ball of paper clay, and flatten it into an oval face shape; let dry. Roll a ¼" ball, and elongate it to form the nose. Press it onto the center of the face, blending the outer edges until they're smooth. Make indentations for nostrils with a toothpick. Roll two ¼" balls for the cheeks. Place one ball on each side of the nose, blending the outer edges into the face; let the clay dry.

### Paint the Face
Paint the face flesh color. With ivory, paint an almond shape for each eye. With gray, paint a circle for an iris in the center of each almond shape. Paint a small circle of black for the pupil in the center of each gray circle. Highlight the pupils with small dots of ivory. Use a liner brush to outline the tops of the eyes with black. Dry-brush the cheeks with red. Then dry-brush the upper cheeks with ivory; let the paint dry. Make a wash of 4 parts water and 1 part antiquing glaze; brush it onto the face; let the glaze dry. Spray the face with acrylic sealer.

### Add the Hair and Beard
Refer to the instructions for each individual ornament or the box. Glue the face in place before applying the hair or the beard.

the sprig and berry to the hair. Attach the wire hanger to the ornament, and trim it with a raffia bow; glue the bell to the bow.

**Star:** Cut the edges from the doily, and divide the doily into four pieces of equal length. Brush the scalloped pieces with fabric stiffener, and place one piece on each of four points of the star. Paint the wooden star gold; spray the star and batting with glitter. Glue the Santa face to the star 1½" below the point without a doily. Glue the beard and hair to the face. Spray the evergreen sprig and berry with glitter. Glue the sprig and berry to the hair. Glue two beneath the beard. Attach the wire hanger to the ornament, and trim with a raffia bow. Glue the wooden star to the bow; glue the pearl button to the star.

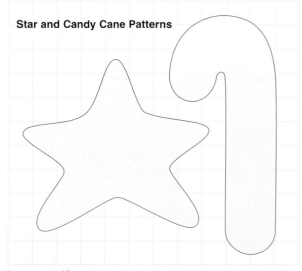

**Star and Candy Cane Patterns**

1 square = 1"

# SWEET SENSATIONS

For generations, tasty Better Homes and Gardens®
treats like these have brought people together.
Colorful banbury tarts beckon little fingers,
and classic almond crescents practically glow with
deliciousness. Once you make these irresistible delights,
they're sure to become a holiday tradition.

Recipes, ingredients, and baking equipment have
changed through the years, but cookies have always
been a family favorite at Christmas. Shown (clockwise
from upper left) are **Mint Meltaways, Sour Cream
Pastries, Kris Kringles, Boston Cookies, Banbury
Tarts,** and **Spice Diamonds.**

Better Homes and Gardens

10 Cents

...e Cakes

...4 eggs

...tter          Flour enough to roll

...and sugar to a cream, then

...gs and flour. Keep dough

...e while rolling out and

...cutting them in the oven

...n the yolk of an egg and

...nuts. Bake slowly at 250°

...ugh in the

...the morning.

In the photograph, *opposite*, nuts, raisins, and currants give spicy **Boston Cookies,** *left*, an old-fashioned chewiness. Shaped with a simple cutter shape, **Butter Cakes,** *right*, are crisp and buttery.

# LOOKING BACK ~ 75 YEARS AGO

Although the first stand-mounted mixer was the 1920 KitchenAid, it wasn't until the Sunbeam Mixmaster appeared on the market in 1930 that there was widespread acceptance of the electric mixer as a necessity in the American kitchen. It was slow to take hold, perhaps because even in the mid-1920s, many American homes didn't yet have electricity.

The country was still largely rural. It was no wonder, then, that the original recipe for Boston Cookies called for "a scant cupful of butter" and noted that "half chicken fat or lard may be used." Most folks kept chickens, and a good share of them kept pigs, too.

Whether one lived in the country or the city, there was general consensus about one thing—what made a good home. Mrs. John D. Sherman, president of the General Federation of Women's Clubs, laid out her prescription for "The Ideal Home" in the December 1924 issue of *Better Homes and Gardens*® magazine. Its vital elements included children, work, cheerfulness, efficiency, religion, honesty, and "music, good pictures, and books."

She left out just one thing. "A well-filled cookie jar is always an asset and is a necessity at Christmastime when the children are holidaying and young visitors are numerous," mused another writer in the December 1924 issue. "One always feels so comfortable, too, at afternoon teatime, if one has a liberal supply of crisp, tempting cookies on hand." Some things never change.

## BOSTON COOKIES

- ¾ cup butter or margarine
- 1 cup granulated sugar
- ½ cup packed brown sugar
- 1 teaspoon baking powder
- 1 teaspoon ground cinnamon
- ½ teaspoon baking soda
- ½ teaspoon ground nutmeg
- ⅛ teaspoon salt
- 3 eggs
- 3¼ cups all-purpose flour
- 1 cup chopped pecans or walnuts
- ½ cup golden raisins
- ½ cup currants
  Pecan or walnut halves
  Granulated sugar

■ Beat the butter or margarine in a bowl with an electric mixer on medium to high speed for 30 seconds. Add the 1 cup granulated sugar, brown sugar, baking powder, cinnamon, baking soda, nutmeg, and salt.

Beat until combined. Add the eggs and beat until well combined. Beat in as much of the flour as you can. Stir in any remaining flour, and the chopped nuts, raisins, and currants with a wooden spoon.

■ Drop by teaspoons 2 inches apart onto a greased cookie sheet. Top each with a nut half, and sprinkle with additional granulated sugar. Bake in a 375° oven about 10 minutes or until the edges are lightly browned. Cool on wire racks. Makes about 70.

## BUTTER CAKES

- 1 cup butter (no substitutes)
- 1 cup sugar
- 1 teaspoon vanilla
- 2 eggs
- 3¼ cups all-purpose flour
- 1 egg yolk
- ⅓ cup finely chopped almonds

■ Beat the butter in a mixing bowl with an electric mixer on medium speed for 30 seconds. Add the sugar and vanilla, and beat at high speed until fluffy. Add the eggs; and beat until well combined. Beat in as much of the flour as you can with the mixer. Stir in the remaining flour with a wooden spoon. Divide the dough in half. Cover and chill until easy to handle (about 1 hour).

■ Roll each half of the dough to ⅛" thickness on a lightly floured surface. Cut with a 2½" scalloped round or tree-shape cookie cutter. Place 1" apart on an ungreased cookie sheet. Beat together the egg yolk and 1 tablespoon water; brush over the cookies. Sprinkle with almonds. Bake in a 375° oven for 6 to 8 minutes or until the edges are firm and the bottoms are very lightly browned. Cool on wire racks. Makes 72.

# LOOKING BACK ~ 50 YEARS AGO

"If you are like most people," began a 1945 article in *Better Homes and Gardens*® magazine, "the first thing on your postwar shopping list is House." Thousands of young men came home after World War II, eager to settle down, marry, and start families. It was a new era for America, a time to start over and move ahead. That dream came to be all about home.

Everyone—including the editors of *Better Homes and Gardens*—was speculating about the dream house of the future. One article of the era, "Preview of Your Kitchen to Come," anticipated a kitchen that was "smooth, clutter-free, colorful, and everything enclosed and built-in." Another piece was called "Your Kitchen Should Have What You Need, Where You Need It, When You Need It." The article noted that, "Most would do more baking if it were not a tiring marathon from one part of the kitchen to another; to make baking more fun, less work, we concentrate tools and ingredients for a one-spot job." One-spot job or not, classic cookies such as Almond Crescents and Kris Kringles were baked in kitchens all across the country and filled holiday cookie jars with sweet dreams.

## ALMOND CRESCENTS
1   cup butter (no substitutes)
¼   cup sifted powdered sugar
1   tablespoon water
2   teaspoons vanilla
2   cups all-purpose flour
1   cup chopped blanched almonds
    Sifted powdered sugar

■ Beat the butter in a bowl with an electric mixer on medium speed for 30 seconds. Add the ¼ cup powdered sugar and beat until combined. Add the water and vanilla; beat until well combined. Beat in as much of the flour as you can. Stir in any remaining flour and the almonds.

■ Using a scant tablespoon for each cookie, form the dough into crescents about 2" long. Place on an ungreased cookie sheet. Bake in a 325° oven for 20 minutes or until bottoms are lightly browned. While the cookies are still warm, roll them in powdered sugar. Roll again in powdered sugar before serving. Makes 48.

## KRIS KRINGLES
1   cup shortening
½   cup sugar
1   egg
2   teaspoons lemon juice
2   cups all-purpose flour

4   teaspoons finely shredded orange peel
2   teaspoons finely shredded lemon peel
2   slightly beaten egg whites
1¾   cups finely chopped walnuts
    Sliced red or green candied cherries

■ Beat the shortening in a bowl with an electric mixer on medium speed for 30 seconds. Add the sugar and ½ teaspoon salt; beat until combined. Add the egg and lemon juice; beat until combined. Stir in the flour and orange and lemon peels.

■ Shape into 1-inch balls. Dip in egg whites; roll lightly in nuts. Place on a greased cookie sheet; place slices of candied cherry on top of each cookie. Bake in a 325° oven about 20 minutes or until the bottoms are lightly browned. Makes 40.

## BANBURY TARTS
¼   cup raisins, chopped
3   tablespoons sugar
1   slightly beaten egg yolk
1   tablespoon drained maraschino cherries, chopped
1   tablespoon chopped walnuts
1   tablespoon fine dry bread crumbs
1½   teaspoons finely shredded lemon peel

2   teaspoons lemon juice
    Plain Pastry
1   egg white
1   tablespoon water
    Sugar

■ Combine the raisins, sugar, egg yolk, cherries, walnuts, bread crumbs, lemon peel, and lemon juice in a bowl.

■ Roll each half of the pastry on lightly floured surface to ⅛" thickness. Cut 3" rounds with a fluted cookie cutter. Place 1 teaspoon of the filling on each round, and moisten the edges of the pastry with water. Fold each round in half, pressing the edges with the tines of a fork to seal. Combine the egg white and water. Brush over the tops of the tarts and sprinkle lightly with the sugar. Place the tarts on an ungreased cookie sheet. Bake in a 425° oven for 10 to 12 minutes. Cool the tarts on a wire rack. Makes 48.

**Plain Pastry:** Stir together 1½ cups of all-purpose flour and ¼ teaspoon of salt. Cut in ½ cup of shortening until the mixture is the size of small peas. Slowly add 4 to 5 tablespoons of cold water, tossing until the mixture is moistened. Shape the mixture into a ball. Divide the pastry into half.

**Banbury Tarts,** *left,* are brushed with egg whites and sprinkled with sugar for sparkly tops. Orange and lemon peels give **Kris Kringles,** *center,* a pleasant citrus flavor. To easily coat the **Almond Crescent** cookies, *right,* place powdered sugar in a plastic bag, add a few crescents, and seal the bag and shake.

**Sour Cream Pastries**, *left,* are easy to fill with apricots. Finely crushed mints flavor the **Mint Meltaways,** *center.* **Spice Diamonds**, *right,* are piped with a squiggle of icing, and sprinkled with a little colored sugar.

# LOOKING BACK ~ 25 YEARS AGO

◆

The times, they were a changin'. A quarter century ago, the pages of *Better Homes and Gardens*® magazine featured one ad for a flowered teakettle designed by hippie artist Peter Max and pages that acknowledged the cultural turmoil caused by the conflict in Vietnam. *Better Homes and Gardens* was a bastion of stability. "The more things change, the more Christmas remains the same," began "The American Family Christmas" in the December 1971 issue. Christmas is "an oasis of calm and continuity in a troubled world."

One of the comforts in an uncertain world is familiar and soothing food—particularly something sweet. The editors knew that well, and that Christmas offered up what they called "a sugarplum assortment of our traditional recipes," including Sour Cream Pastries, Spice Diamonds, and Mint Meltaways.

## SOUR CREAM PASTRIES

- 1 cup butter (no substitutes)
- 2 cups all-purpose flour
- ½ cup dairy sour cream
- 1 beaten egg yolk
- ½ cup apricot preserves
- ½ cup flaked coconut
- ¼ cup finely chopped pecans
  Granulated or powdered sugar
  (about 4 teaspoons)

■ Cut the butter into the flour in a mixing bowl until the mixture resembles fine crumbs. Combine the sour cream and egg yolk; stir into the flour mixture, using your hands to mix well. Form into a ball. If the dough seems soft, cover and chill for a few hours or overnight.

■ Snip any large pieces of apricot in preserves. Combine the preserves, coconut, and pecans in a small bowl. Set aside.

■ Divide the dough into fourths. Roll one portion at a time into a 10-inch circle on a lightly floured surface. Spread each circle thinly with one-fourth of the filling mixture, leaving a 2-inch circle in the center without filling. Using a fluted pastry wheel or a sharp knife, cut each circle into 12 wedges. Starting from the wide end, roll up each wedge to the point. Place the pastries point-side down on an ungreased cookie sheet. Sprinkle the tops with granulated or powdered sugar. Bake in a 350° oven for 18 to 20 minutes or until lightly browned. Cool on wire racks. Makes 4.

## MINT MELTAWAYS

- 1 cup butter (no substitutes)
- 1 cup finely crushed butter mints
  (about 5 ounces)
- 2 cups all-purpose flour
- 1 tablespoon sugar

■ Beat the butter in a bowl with an electric mixer on medium speed for 30 seconds. Add the mints and beat until fluffy. Beat in as much of the flour as you can. Stir in any remaining flour. Cover and chill for 1 hour.

■ Roll or pat the dough on waxed paper into a 9" square. Sprinkle with sugar. Cut into 1½" squares. Place on an ungreased cookie sheet. Using a small cookie cutter, press a design on the surface of dough.

■ Bake in a 325° oven for 12 to 15 minutes or until the bottoms are pale golden brown. Cool on wire racks. Makes 36.

---

## SPICE DIAMONDS

- ½ cup butter or margarine
- ½ cup sugar
- ½ teaspoon baking soda
- ½ teaspoon ground cinnamon
- ¼ teaspoon salt
- ¼ teaspoon ground ginger
- ¼ teaspoon ground nutmeg
- ¼ teaspoon ground cardamon
- ¼ teaspoon ground cloves
- 1 egg
- 1 tablespoon molasses
- 1½ cups all-purpose flour
- ½ teaspoon finely shredded
  orange peel
- ½ teaspoon finely shredded
  lemon peel
  Powdered Sugar Icing
  Colored decorating sugar

■ Beat the butter or margarine in a mixing bowl, with an electric mixer on medium to high speed, for 30 seconds. Add the sugar, baking soda, cinnamon, salt, ginger, nutmeg, cardamom, and cloves. Beat until combined. Add the egg and molasses. Beat until well combined. Beat in as much of the flour as you can. Stir in the orange and lemon peels, and the remaining flour with a wooden spoon. Divide the dough in half. Cover and chill for about 1 hour.

■ Roll half of the dough at a time on a lightly floured surface to ⅛" thickness. Cut the dough into diamond shapes (about 2x1") using a knife or rotary cutter with a scalloped edge. Place the shapes 1" apart on an ungreased cookie sheet. Bake in a 350° oven for 6 to 8 minutes or until the edges are lightly browned. To serve, pipe with Powdered Sugar Icing; and sprinkle with the colored sugar. Makes about 100.

■ **Powdered Sugar Icing:** Combine 1 cup of sifted powdered sugar and enough milk (about 1 tablespoon) to make a sufficient amount for drizzling consistency.

# COLLECTIBLES
## *on* PARADE

FILLED WITH MEMORIES
AND SPECIAL SENTIMENTS,
YOUR CHRISTMAS COLLECTIONS
DESERVE PROUD DISPLAY.
THE PRESENTATION
CAN BE AS STRIKING AS THE
ITEMS THEMSELVES
WHEN YOU DECK THE HALLS
WITH PIECES THAT
COMMEMORATE THE SEASON.

Gather some of your favorite Santa treasures,
and line them along shelves and ledges in a
gallery of great collectibles.

# COLLECTIBLES
## ON
# *Parade*

CHRISTMAS SENTIMENT STIRS ALL
THROUGH THE HOUSE WITH THESE CREATIVE
WAYS TO DISPLAY YOUR TREASURES.

A s you unwrap handfuls of heirloom trinkets and antique ornaments, put them in places of prominence. Hang them from hooks, dangle them from drawers, and bunch them in bowls. Embellish your displays with attractive backdrops of holiday greenery, colorful ribbons, and poignant poinsettias. Drape surfaces with colorful background fabric, and use light to showcase special scenes. In family rooms, bedrooms, and even bathrooms, spread reminders of Christmas throughout your home—and surround your friends and family with the spirit of the season.

Mix and match items that go together, like this nature-loving Santa and weathered birdhouse, *top left.* A soft bed of evergreens and fallen pinecones create a natural backdrop.

An antique pop-up book stands on its own, *bottom left,* with engaging colors and details. Create single settings like this to showcase your best pieces.

Invite entertaining holiday pastimes by displaying nostalgic books and magazines, *opposite, top left,* on a coffee table or end table.

Dolls and ornaments interspersed among ordinary objects are gentle reminders of Christmas, *opposite, top right.*

This Santa convention beckons admirers to come close, *opposite bottom.* Some of the Santas hang whimsically from a wreath.